DATE DUE

AP 04 '14			
DEC 10 '18			

Everyday Life in Early India

The Buddha's descent to earth. From Amarāvatī

Everyday Life in
EARLY INDIA

MICHAEL EDWARDES

Drawings by Oliver Williams

B. T. BATSFORD LTD London
G. P. PUTNAM'S SONS New York

First published 1969

Text © Michael Edwardes, 1969
Illustrations © B. T. Batsford Ltd, 1969

7134 1682 3

Printed and bound in Great Britain by
Jarrold and Sons Ltd, Norwich and London,
for the publishers

B. T. BATSFORD LTD
4 Fitzhardinge Street, Portman Square, London

G. P. PUTNAM'S SONS
200 Madison Avenue, New York, NY 10016

Contents

Acknowledgment   viii

The Illustrations   ix

Preface   xiii

Note on the pronunciation of Indian words   xiv

Introduction: Discovering Early India   I

1   Strife, Quarrel, Dissension, and War   4

2   The Framework of Living   20

3   The Daily Round   53

4   War   140

5   Arts and Sciences   145

Index   169

Acknowledgment

The author and publishers wish to thank the following for the illustrations appearing in this book: Arpad Elfer for fig. 89; Barnaby's Picture Library for fig. 28; the City of Birmingham for fig. 93; the Trustees of the British Museum for figs. 17 and 71; J. Allan Cash for fig. 97; the Government of India, Department of Archaeology for figs. 4, 7 and 47; the National Museum, New Delhi, for fig. 92; the Secretary of State for Foreign and Commonwealth Affairs for fig. 65; the Swiss Foundation for Alpine Research and Popperfoto for fig. 9; Popperfoto for fig. 81; W. Suschitzky for figs. 33 and 88; D. B. Taraporevala Sons & Co., Bombay, for figs. 20, 38 and 80; the Victoria and Albert Museum for figs. 3, 46, 51 and 75; and Thames and Hudson Ltd., publishers of *Indian Temples and Sculpture*, 1959, for the frontispiece.

The Illustrations

The Buddha's descent to earth. From Amarāvatī   *frontispiece*

1 Seal from the Indus valley   5
2 India *c.* 200 BC   7
3 Head of the Buddha from Gandhāra   9
4 Jina Mahāvīra   10
5 The Maurya emperor, Aśoka   13
6 Demetrius wearing elephant head-dress of India   15
7 Statue of a Kushana king   17
8 Signature of Harṣa from a copperplate inscription   19
9 The Himālayas   21
10 A sacred island in the river Brahmaputra   23
11 Two brāhmans seated before the king   25
12 A *mleccha* and outcaste seated on winged lions   29
13 An Amazon guard   31
14 Children learning the sacred texts   34
15 The five heroes of the *Mahābhārata* and their wife, Draupadi   38
16 A brāhman begging for food   39
17 Concubines   41
18 A king receiving tribute   45
19 A royal official   49
20 Reconstruction of an Indian village   53
21 Women with children in front of a village house   54
22 A rattan table in the form of an hour-glass   55

23 An earthenware water pot with goblet   55
24 A *yakṣa* plucking mangoes   56
25 Humped bulls   57
26 An antelope caught in a hunter's trap   58
27 Two types of plough   59
28 A herdsman with his cattle   61
29 A woman carrying a basket   62
30 A spice seller's shop   63
31 A covered bullock cart   66
32 A *nāga* king and queen   69
33 A *yakṣa* from the East Gate at Sānchī   70
34 A sacred tree protected by a fence   71
35 A *gandharva* in flight   72
36 A *vidyādhara* carrying off a woman   73
37 An assembly of demons   75
38 Reconstruction of the main gateway of a town   77
39 Town houses   78
40 The top view of a lamp   80
41 A girl on a swing   81
42 A stylised lotus flower   82
43 A grove of trees   83
44 A snake-charmer and cobra   84
45 A woman carrying a child on her hip   85
46 A woman's jewelry   85
47 A seller of curds   87
48 A young man choosing a garland   88
49 Scales   89
50 Bactrian camels   91
51 An Indian ship   93
52 Two donors   94

53 An upper-class bedroom   96
54 A game of dice   97
55–8 Four types of kiss   98–9
59 A woman with a parrot and cage   100
60 Courtesans and companions   101
61 Servants husking and winnowing rice and grinding spices   105
62 Two wrestlers   106
63 Acrobats forming a pyramid   107
64 State elephant   109
65 The Seven Gems, signs of a Universal King   111
66 The royal horse   112
67 The king and his ministers in a chariot   113
68 The royal kitchen   114
69 Two peacocks   115
70 Royal insignia, the fly whisk and umbrella   116
71 The king in his harem   117
72 The guardian of the harem   119
73 Hair curlers   120
74 Decorated ivory combs   120
75 A princess at her toilet   121
76 A concubine paddling in a waterfall   122
77 A king dining   125
78 A hermit outside his hut   129
79 A hermitage   130
80 Reconstruction of Sānchī   131
81 Carpentry simulated in stone. Chaitya Hall   133
82 The Three Jewels   135
83 The Buddha begging for his food   137
84 Battle scenes from the *Mahābhārata*   141
85 A warrior with a spear and sword   143

86 The royal bodyguard and the king in his palanquin   144
87 The distribution of the relics of Buddha   145
88 North Gateway at Sānchī   147
89 Panorama of Ajantā caves   149
90 Aśokan capital from Sārnāth   151
91 Greek columns in a sculpture from Mathurā   152
92 Seated Buddha from Sārnāth   153
93 A Buddha made by the 'lost-wax' method   155
94 Antelopes from Māmallapuram   157
95 Musicians   159
96 Dance poses   160
97 An iron pillar from Meharaulī   165

Preface

This book looks at everyday life and the background to it over a period of roughly a thousand years, from around the third century BC to the eighth century AD. Admittedly, this is an unusually long period of time, but any shorter one, by concentrating on a particular reign or area, would have been misleading. It should hardly be necessary to say that, in the space available, it has not been possible to cover all aspects of life or to examine any of them in depth. This work is an introduction to a complex and fascinating subject—and no more. It is designed for the intelligent, non-specialist reader, not for the scholar, and I make no apology for that. Much of the background to life in early India as it is described in the following pages has necessarily been simplified, though not, I think, over-simplified.

Furthermore, in the case of Indian religious ideas and practice, I have, so to speak, kept to the well lighted and main streets and have not gone dashing down those inviting side alleys so dear to the specialist. I do not believe that the reader will be misled by the absence of much recondite material. Such material is available in a wide range of highly specialised works. I have not listed any of these, however, as I prefer to recommend anyone who wishes to go further into the cultural and political history of early India to begin with what is, I believe, the best work on the subject by an academic authority and one which is both scholarly and easy to read—A. L. Basham's *The Wonder that was India* (London and New York, new edition 1967). Professor Basham's book contains an extensive bibliography.

The drawings which illustrate the present work are all based upon contemporary sources and, in the main, upon surviving paintings and sculpture.

Note on the pronunciation of Indian words

Indian words used in this book are spelt according to the standard system of transliteration at present in general use. This method calls for a great number of diacritical signs, which can be very confusing to the ordinary reader. However, without these signs it is impossible to give a clear idea of the proper prounuciation of Sanskrit and Pāli words. The ordinary reader needs only an approximate guide, and that is all that is given here.

The vowels ā, ī, ū, e, ai, o, and au, are pronounced as in the English words calm, machine, rule, prey, time, go, and cow, respectively. A, i, u as in cut, bit and bush. Ṛ is like the ri in rich, th and ph as in pothole and shepherd. C is pronounced as the ch in church. Ś and ṣ as in sh in sheep. The ordinary reader need not worry about other diacriticals.

Introduction: Discovering Early India

How do we know how people lived and thought in India during the period covered by this book? A partial answer would be because, to a surprising extent, the same way of life still exists today. Unlike the other great civilisations of the ancient world—Egypt, Mesopotamia, and Greece —that of India does not have to be entirely dug up out of the ground. Only China, a continuous civilisation until our own times, offers any parallel. Archaeology in India supplies proof of something that can be seen in action, for the civilisation of early India is still very much alive. This does not, of course, mean that there have been no changes, no new institutions, no new customs. Because of the discoveries of archaeologists, epigraphers, and social anthropologists, we know that there *have* been. But these changes have been so slow in coming about that it is possible to find customs of great antiquity co-existing, without friction, with the most recent. Even an ordinary Indian is aware, not so much of the antiquity of the traditions he cherishes and lives by, but of their continuity.

When the first Europeans arrived in India they discovered a civilisation fully conscious of its great age and apparent lack of change. It was a civilisation with a strong sense of the past but no sense of history (in the way in which it was defined in the West) because it had no need of it. Culturally speaking, the past and the present were identical and knowledge of the rise and fall of kings was of no real interest. This rejection of history, of dates, explanations of motives, and so on, did not merely reflect the universal indifference of the illiterate. It was an attitude shared by kings, who did not even bother to leave precise records of their own achievements—real or imagined—on the monuments they erected.

Without the need for history, there were no historians. There were chroniclers, but as we can see in those of their works which have survived, they turned real events into myths. This came about because Indian literature of all kinds was highly conventional, carefully observant of traditional forms. Conformism is a fundamental characteristic of the Indian mind and there seems to have been no wish to deviate from tradition.

I

All this has made it very difficult to plot the course of early Indian history with any precision. Much of what is now accepted as the chronology of events is based only upon deduction.

Fortunately, the disdain of Indian writers—and sculptors—for *historical* fact did not extend to a total rejection of reality, to an indifference to things seen. Descriptions of places were frequently conventional. A king's palace, for example, was portrayed with the splendour traditionally suitable to the *idea* of a king's palace, rather than that of any specific building. But quite often the writer would add realistic details about the homes and the surroundings of lesser men. Authors of the tales and verses which were the stock-in-trade of travelling story-tellers filled their work with fragments of everyday life. Sculptors and painters were dependent on reality for the background of their work. With their aid it is possible to reconstruct much of the material of life in the village, the town, and the palace of the king. There are also contemporary descriptions by foreigners, mostly Greek and Chinese. From these, together with bas-reliefs, mural paintings and inscriptions, and religious and secular texts, life in early India can be reconstructed—and compared with life today.

But the past can only be recovered in the most general terms. Documentation, where it exists, is rarely concerned with identifiable places and historical persons. It almost always describes ideal situations rather than real ones. For example, we still do not know—and it is unlikely that we ever will—whether that indispensable work, the *Arthaśāstra*, ascribed to Kauṭilya, is a truthful description of the Mauryan state or not. Even archaeology cannot help us directly because the secular buildings of rich and poor alike were built of perishable materials and have long crumbled into dust. They can only be re-created from art and literature. Even then, it is often only the works of foreign visitors that give us a description of a particular building or of a precise place. There is, in fact, a unique anonymity about India's past. Even where persons *are* named there can be solid doubts about when they lived or even whether they actually existed at all. The mass of early Indian literature bears no author's name. Even in works that do, nothing of the author's character can be found in them.

With all these difficulties in the way, truth must depend upon the choice of material used. The discovery of India's past was, until recently, the achievement of European scholars who brought to their interpretations the values—and prejudices—of their own civilisation. Translations made of early Indian literature were almost entirely confined to sacred texts, both Buddhist and Hindu. From these was created a peculiarly contra-dictory image of India and the Indians. Some scholars saw India as the repository of great spiritual truths which, in some manner not too closely defined, might act as an antidote to the growing materialism of the West. Others, usually Christians influenced by missionary ideas, saw Indians oppressed by the evils of caste, and dominated by a gloomy philosophy in which acceptance of famine and disease was a virtue. On this foundation was built a view still with us—of a god-ridden, lazy people unwilling to enjoy life and lacking any desire to improve it. Anyone acquainted with modern India knows how untrue this view is today. It was also untrue of early India. The law books make it quite obvious that everybody was by no means virtuous and conformist, that gambling, for example, was passionately enjoyed by all classes. Even though it was expressly forbidden, people of one caste married people of another. Popular literature reveals that life within the general framework of a highly formal, though still evolving, society was as happy, as unrestrained, and as gay as material circumstances would allow.

The world revealed by the sacred texts and the treatises on law and government reflect one aspect of early Indian civilisation, folk literature another. Both pictures display part of the truth and, together, reflect reality. What follows has been constructed from the widest range of sources to give a view of a civilisation, refined, brilliant, lusty, and incomparable.

1 Strife, Quarrel, Dissension, and War

According to Hindu chronology, a new age (*yuga*) began in 3102 BC. It had been preceded by three others. The first was one in which men and women were born virtuous and remained so. Those which followed had been characterised by a steady decline in morality and behaviour. The new age, called the *Kali-yuga*, was a dark age in which strife, quarrel, dissension, and war were the order of things. Certainly, the period covered by this book is one of frequent anarchy and social disturbance, although there are long periods of political stability under great and powerful kings.

War and the creation and destruction of kingdoms are as much part of the lives of ordinary people as their religion, art, and literature, their social activities, their planting and sowing, buying and selling. Though a good deal of our knowledge of early Indian history is extremely vague, there is plenty of evidence of great invasions, of the rise and fall of empires, of periods of violence and anarchy. But the exploration of early Indian civilisation has suffered from too many narrow specialists, uninterested in political and social history. Because of this, there is a widespread belief that early Indian civilisation was interested only in matters of the spirit.

From archaeological excavations, we now know that—somewhere around 2000 BC—very sophisticated cities existed in the valley of the Indus river in what is today West Pakistan. The civilisation of these cities had strong connections with those to the north and, in particular, with Mesopotamia. About 1500 BC these cities were attacked by semi-nomad barbarians known as Āryans, who brought with them a language, a religion, and other cultural elements which formed the foundations of early Indian civilisation. The Āryan invasion of India was not a single event but a series, covering centuries and involving more than one tribe. The invaders did not like living in cities, and their settlements were little villages with buildings of wood and reeds. Among the Āryans who entered India was a group of tribes whose priests had composed a large number of sacred hymns for use in religious rites. Among these tribes, that of the Bharatas (the word *bharat* is used today by Hindu political parties as

4

1 A seal from the Indus
   valley

anothe r word for 'India') carefully handed down their hymns by word of
mouth. These hymns are known as the *Rig-Veda*, the most sacred of
Hindu texts. The Vedic hymns are still declaimed at weddings and funerals,
as alive today as they were 3000 years ago.

This sacred literature tells us very little about great events or social
conditions. It is, however, clear that the invaders were still fighting against
the people they had driven out of the Indus cities. The Āryans, who were
light-skinned, described their enemies as dark and ugly, and it is here that
can be found the origin of the caste-system, for the Sanskrit word *varṇa*
—which is often wrongly translated as 'caste'—means colour. When the
Āryans entered India they already had class-divisions, between the nobility
and the ordinary tribesmen. Once they settled down, class-divisions
hardened to exclude the indigenous peoples whom the Āryans called *dāsa*,
or slave, and Āryans who intermarried with them. By about 500 BC,
which is the generally accepted date for the end of the Vedic period,
society was divided into four great classes: the priests (*brāhmana*), warriors
(*kṣatriya*), peasants (*vaiśya*), and serfs (*śūdra*). These general classes survive
today. The four divisions were said to be of divine origin.

The Āryans were not obsessed by religion. They had very few of the
prohibitions found in later times. Though there are references in their
literature to a ban on the killing of cows, this seems to have been purely

5

for economic reasons as cattle were used as a sort of currency. It is also quite certain that cows and oxen *were* killed for food. The Āryans were addicted to two rather potent liquors. They liked music and singing, dancing-girls and gambling. One of the very few surviving secular poems is a gambler's lament.

The religious ideas of the early Āryans were comparatively simple. There was a great deal of emphasis on sacrifice, for their gods personified the forces of nature and it was therefore necessary to propitiate them. Fortunately, magical phrases (*brahman*) could be used to make the gods allies of men. Sacrifice consisted of pouring a libation of a drink known as *soma*. This drink produced vivid hallucinations; though the plant used in its preparation has not been acceptably identified, it seems to have been a sort of hemp. If this is so, the Āryans had indulged in psychedelic experiences thousands of years before the hippies and flower people of our own times.

The sacred texts are not very precise about the origin of the world, and the idea of a creator was only a vague conception. As for the individual soul and its destiny, though the Āryans had a hell and a heaven, they knew nothing of the rewards for a good life, or of judgement, or of punishment after death.

From about 900 BC onwards a very important change emerged in the attitude to sacrifice. The priests, who were the only people who knew the correct sacred phrases, seem to have developed the full concept of a creator—later called Brahmā—who was sacrificed before the world began, presumably by other gods, and from whose body the universe was produced. The act of sacrifice therefore became a repetition of this first sacrifice. If it were not performed regularly, it was said that the cosmic process would end and chaos return. The priest therefore became greater than any king, the preserver of the world, the most important person in society—and one who could, if he felt like it, destroy his enemies by changing the ritual. This was the beginning of the dominant role of the priest in the Hindu community.

It was about this time also, that new ideas about the individual soul were developed. The idea of transmigration, of the constant rebirth of the soul in a different body, led to the concept of *karma* which argued that what was done in one life affected the next. This highly logical doctrine supplied a purpose for suffering, as well as a reason for each man's position in society. Such a concept was of great political and social value.

6

2 India *c.* 200 BC

SDIANA
TRIA

GĀNDHĀRA

PURUṢAPURA ●
(PESHĀWAR)

● TAXILA

ACHOSIA

HARĀPPĀ ●
THĀNEŚVARA ●
INDRAPRASTHA ●
● MOHENJODARO
MATHURĀ ●

HIMALAYA

R. BRAHMAPUTRA

NEPĀL

R. GANGA

R. YAMUNA

KĀNYAKUBYA (KANAUJ) ●
AYODHYĀ ●

KĀMAMŪRA

R. SINDU
(INDUS)

PRAYĀGA ●
VĀRĀNASĪ ●

SĀRNĀTH ●
● BHĀRHUT

PĀṬALIPUTRA ●
● NĀLANDĀ

GAYA ●

VAṄGĀ

DĀSAPUR ●
SĀNCHĪ ●

● VIDISA (BHILSA)

MAGADHA

SURĀṢTRA

R. NARMADĀ

R. MAHĀNADĪ

NĀSIK ●
ELEPHANTA
KĀRLĪ
BHĀJĀ

AJANTĀ ●
● ELLŪRĀ

MAHĀRĀṢṬRA

R. GODĀVARI

KALIṄGA

R. KRIṢṆĀ

ĀNDHRA

● AMARĀVATĪ

KĀRṆĀṬA

COLA

● MĀMALLAPURAM

● TAÑJUVŪR

MUSIRIS ●

CĒRA
KERALA

● MADURAI

PĀNDYA

LAṄKĀ

The development of these religious ideas coincided with a political expansion eastward down the river Ganges. Apart from archaeological discoveries at the ancient city of Hastināpura, near Delhi, the sources for this period are still almost entirely confined to sacred texts. One battle, not recorded in any contemporary text, probably took place at Kurukṣetra not far from present-day Delhi; a highly exaggerated later description of it is given in the great Indian epic, the *Mahābhārata* (second century A D). The battle was probably fought around the middle of the ninth century B C and may well have been part of a civil war between members of the Kuru tribe. About this time the Āryans set up kingdoms in Kosala and Kāśī (the present-day Vārānāsī, formerly Benares, area). The former is supposed to have been the land of Rāma, the hero of the literary epic, the *Rāmāyaṇa*. Though there are considerable doubts about whether Rāma actually was king of Kosala, his traditional father-in-law, Janaka, king of Videha, was certainly an historical person. On the right bank of the Ganges was the region of Magadha, which had not been fully conquered by the Āryans, and there were a number of other small kingdoms lying between the river Jumna and the borders of Bengal.

The Āryans had by this time settled into a less nomadic life. Their kingdoms had small capital cities and there were the beginnings of administration. People were beginning to acquire a sense of place. Though not all tribal organisation had disappeared, it was breaking up. The later Vedic period saw the breakdown of old systems of kinship, and with it came a sense of insecurity which was reflected in that pessimistic outlook characteristic of times of great social change.

In the new settled administration, the king was becoming all-powerful, surrounding himself with courtiers and officials. New royal sacrifices and special rituals designed to enhance the king's position appear in the sacred texts. Of the sacrifices, the most significant in its consequences was the horse sacrifice. A specially consecrated horse was let loose for a year followed by a band of warriors. Wherever the horse chose to roam, the ruler of the territory was forced either to pay homage to the king who had released it, or fight the warriors. If the horse still wandered free at the end of the year, it was brought back to the king for sacrifice. It can be imagined how many unnecessary wars were fought because of the horse.

New developments in religion during this period have already been mentioned. During it, Indian life and thought took on the general pattern they have followed ever since. Kings and priests grew in power and

3 Head of the Buddha
from Gandhāra

emerged slowly out of the anonymous shadows of legend and tradition.
In the sixth century BC true history begins, though it still does not bring
any certainty about dates or accurate descriptions of people. The facts we
do have mainly concern four great kingdoms, Kosala, Magadha, Vatsa,
and Avanti. Most is known, however, about the first two because they
are the scene of the lives and activities of two great religious reformers,
the Buddha and Mahāvīra. Kosala was apparently in decline, but Magadha,
which had not been completely Āryanised, had an efficient ruler in
Bimbisāra (c. 542–c. 490 BC).

It was in those areas in which the Āryans had not fully imposed
Brāhmanism and the rigid division of society into caste, that a liberal

9

4 Jina Mahāvīra

opposition came into being. Undoubtedly, the leaders of the liberation movement, the Buddha and Mahāvīra, had a political as well as a religious purpose. Both certainly wanted to destroy the power of the priests. But their revolt was fundamentally one of the heart, for they wanted to bring to ordinary people a sense of hope and the chance of freedom, not only from the endless cycle of rebirth but from the restrictions of the social order.

Both the Buddha and Mahāvīra were the sons of tribal chieftains in an area across the Ganges, north of Magadha. Both advocated peaceful solutions to the problems of society. The founder of Jainism, Mahāvīra, or 'Great Hero' (c. 540–c. 468 BC), preached asceticism and total non-violence, a doctrine too cold and austere to appeal to a wide number of people. Today there remain in India only a few hundred thousand Jains. But the Buddha, 'Awakened' or 'Enlightened' (c. 563–c. 483 BC), was to have a profound effect not only in India but in the whole of eastern Asia. Undoubtedly the Buddha was, even if judged by this alone, the greatest Indian of all time. The basis of his teaching was that all life is suffering and that the source of this suffering is desire. If desire can be eliminated, then so can suffering. To the Buddha there was no caste, no inequality between man and man. Both asceticism and luxury were condemned, for moderation in all things was the ideal of the 'Middle Way'. Through virtuous activity, the cycle of rebirth could be broken and the soul pass into *nirvāṇa*, a state of bliss. The Buddha accepted the gods of Brāhmanism, but held that they, too, were in need of salvation. The Buddha's achievement was to lay the foundations of a revolution which was to be brought about by others.

The teachings of the Buddha and Mahāvīra were not the only examples of new thinking in their time. Brāhmanism—in self-defence—absorbed the cults of various gods, many of them of tribal or local origin. But it was Buddhism which triumphed in Magadha and from there spread across northern India.

About 490 B C, seven years before the death of the Buddha, Bimbisāra of Magadha was murdered by his son Ajātaśatru, who expanded the kingdom by going to war with his uncle Prasenajit, king of Kosala, and gaining control of Kāśī. Prasenajit himself was deposed by his son, who, like Ajātaśatru, had dreams of empire. During the course of expansion, he destroyed the tribe into which the Buddha had been born. Both the kings of Magadha were in diplomatic contact with the empire of the Persian Achaemenid, Darius I, which extended over part of north-western India. Young men were sent from Magadha to the important centre of learning and trade there, Takṣaśilā (Taxila), and undoubtedly they and Magadha were considerably influenced by Persian ideas. Very little is known of the later years of Ajātaśatru, but he certainly created the most powerful empire India had then known, its territories covering both banks of the Ganges from Vārāṇasī to the borders of Bengal. Expansion undoubtedly continued after his death, for, in the fourth century B C when facts once again become fairly clear, the empire of Magadha with its capital of Pāṭaliputra (present-day Patna) covered the whole of northern India with the exception of Rajasthan, Sind, Punjab, and the north-west.

In the middle of the fourth century B C Magadha was ruled by Mahāpadma Nanda, who expanded his territories as far as the Bay of Bengal. On his death there was considerable confusion, and what actually happened remains obscured by legend. In 330 BC Alexander of Macedon defeated Darius III and began his conquest of the Persian empire. Six years later he crossed the Indus river, meeting strong opposition from a king of the Punjab whom the Greeks called Porus (possibly from the Sanskrit Paurava). Porus was defeated. When Alexander retreated, he was left in charge of the Punjab as a vassal king. Alexander's retreat and unexpected death in 323 BC left a power vacuum in north-western India.

According to classical sources, an Indian called Sandrocottus had supported Alexander and tried to persuade him to attack Magadha. For various reasons, Alexander refused. Finally, Sandrocottus is said to have overthrown certain of the Greek garrisons left behind in India and established a great empire of his own. This 'Sandrocottus' is the Chandragupta Maurya mentioned in Indian sources. Whether or not the story of his encounter with Alexander is true, he undoubtedly overthrew the Nanda dynasty in Magadha and expelled the Greek garrisons. The exact date has not been established, though it was certainly between 324 and 313 BC. According to Indian tradition, Chandragupta was wisely advised by his minister Kauṭilya, who is the alleged author of the *Arthaśāstra* or 'Treatise on Polity'. The text which has survived is not by Kauṭilya, though it does contain very valuable material about the Maurya empire.

About 300 BC, one of Alexander's generals, Seleucus Nicator—who had established himself in the Asian provinces of his former master's empire —moved eastwards and fought a battle with Chandragupta in which Seleucus, if not actually defeated, came off so badly that he gave up the attempt to reimpose Greek rule in north-western India and was also forced to hand over parts of what is now Afghanistan to Chandragupta. The two kings celebrated the peace with a matrimonial alliance; according to tradition, Chandragupta married a Greek princess. Seleucus appointed an ambassador to the Maurya empire and it is to this envoy, Megasthenes that we owe a description of Chandragupta's court. The original work has been lost but portions of it survive, in quotation, in the works of many Greek and Latin authors. Megasthenes' record is the first by a foreign traveller. From it we learn of a highly organised state. Chandragupta lived in great luxury in a vast palace built of wood. He went in constant fear of assassination and was supposed never to sleep two consecutive nights in the same room. A ubiquitous secret service was perpetually on the watch for conspiracies.

According to Jaina tradition, Chandragupta abdicated, became a Jaina

5 The Maurya emperor,
Aśoka

monk, and starved himself to death in a monastery in what is today
Mysore. Whatever the truth of this, he reigned for twenty-four years
before being succeeded by his son, Bindusāra. Very little is known about
the second Maurya emperor, apart from a story that he asked Antiochus I,
king of Syria, for gifts of figs, wine, and a sophist. Antiochus is reported
to have sent the figs and the wine, but to have said that he did not trade in
philosophers. It seems probable that Bindusāra extended the empire to the
Deccan. He was succeeded, about 269 BC, by his son Aśoka. Though there
are no known foreign reports about Aśoka, the greatest of the Maurya
rulers, he revealed much of his own character in a series of edicts, probably
written by himself, which were engraved on rocks and pillars all over
India.

These tell us that eight years after his consecration as emperor, having
conquered the kingdom of Kalinga on the Bay of Bengal with great
violence and brutality, he suddenly realised the inhumanity of what he
had done and, in his repentance, decided to act only with righteousness
(dharma). This meant, in effect, a humane administration and the rejection
of war as a means of conquest. Aśoka was certainly a Buddhist, but he was
not particularly interested in metaphysics. He believed that an enlightened
government was better than a harsh one, and that his example would so
impress other kings that they would accept his moral leadership. Aśoka
was not a pacifist; there is no mention of the army being disbanded. He
retained the death penalty, too, which was only to be abolished by later

13

Indian rulers. He did, however, give up hunting and animals were no longer killed for his table. Though he did not try to force Buddhism on his subjects, it was during his reign that the doctrines of the Buddha began to be diffused outside India. According to tradition a great council of Buddhist priests was held at Pāṭaliputra, when the authorised scriptures were collected, and missionaries sent abroad. It is clear that Aśoka was a man of great ability and authority—a little naïve perhaps, and given to lecturing his subjects. But his state was well ruled, and its economic development vigorously pressed. He is also the first major Indian figure who is convincingly real.

After the death of Aśoka (*c.* 232 BC), his empire fell to pieces. Little is known of his successors apart from their names. About 183 BC, Puṣyamitra Śuṅga, a brāhman general of the last Maurya emperor, assumed the throne by a *coup d'état*. He revived orthodox religion and reinstated ancient sacrifices, including the horse sacrifice. The capital of the new Śuṅga kingdom was at Vidiśā. The state was no longer the strong, centralised monarchy of Aśoka but a collection of vassal kingdoms; in effect, a loose feudal system. The rest of the Maurya empire broke up into independent states. Aśoka's rejection of aggressive war was forgotten and anarchy and violence returned to northern India. So, too, did the Greeks.

About the middle of the third century BC, a number of colonies of Asiatic Greeks, which had been established by Alexander and Seleucus Nicator, had begun to declare themselves independent of the Seleucid empire. One of these, Bactria, came to terms with the then Seleucid emperor and its ruler, Demetrius, entered India early in the second century. He and his successors occupied most of the Indus valley and the Punjab, and one of them, Menander, may well have reached the old Maurya capital of Pāṭaliputra during the course of raids to the east. Other Indo-Greek kingdoms were established in the north-west.

The Śuṅgas, and *their* successors, the Kāṇvas, though unable to hold the Maurya empire together, did manage to keep out the Indo-Greeks. During their rule great cave temples were excavated and decorated with fine sculpture, and many Buddhist stūpas, including those at Bhārhut and Sānchī, were erected. The sculpture, some of which is illustrated in this book, supplies us with a background of the everyday life of the time. Buddhism continued to spread and the Indo-Greek king, Menander, was patron to the Buddhist philosopher Nāgasena. The conversations of these two men survive in a well-known text, *The Questions of Milinda*

14

6 Demetrius wearing the
elephant head-dress of
India

(Menander). There was also great activity within the brāhmanic tradition. Many new sects were founded and a number of Indo-Greeks were attracted by them.

The Indo-Greek—or more properly, perhaps, Greco-Bactrian—kingdoms were, however, nearing their end. Bactria itself was occupied by the Parthians at the beginning of the second half of the second century B C. In central Asia, large bands of nomads were on the move, sent on their way by a variety of causes, climatic and political. A nomadic people, called Yüeh-chi by the Chinese, drove Scythian tribesmen out of their own lands on the borders of Bactria into Bactria itself and then, under mounting pressure, into Iran and India. By the middle of the first century B C, the Scythians, known in India as the Śakas, had conquered much of the northwest. In India the Śuṅgas had been succeeded by the Kāṇvas, who in turn collapsed. Towards the end of the first century B C, a dynasty known as the Pahlavas conquered part of north-west India and ruled for a short period. One of their kings, Gondophernes, is said to have received the apostle Thomas and with him India's first knowledge of the religion of Christianity.

A new name now enters Indian history—that of Kushans (properly Kuṣāṇas). A sub-tribe of the Yüeh-chi, they entered India some time in the first half of the first century A D. Of their kings, the most important was Kaniṣka who ruled (some time between AD 78 and 144) all the western part of India up to Vārānasī as well as large parts of central Asia. Kaniṣka is particularly remembered as a patron of Buddhism. The period of his reign was one of great international, commercial and intellectual activity. The Kushans were in contact with China and with Rome.

Away from the disturbed arena of the north-west, other new kingdoms came into being. In Orissa a great conqueror, Khāravela, appeared. He was a patron of Jainism, but his empire did not last for long. In the Deccan, the Sātāvahanas (or Āndhras) established a dynasty which lasted for 300 years and stretched, in the second century AD, from coast to coast. A Śaka dynasty known as the Western Satraps gained control of Kāthiāwār and Mālwā which it ruled until about AD 388. One of their kings, Rudradāman, can be given the unusual distinction of an accurate date, as an inscription in Sanskrit reveals that he was reigning in the year AD 150.

The far south also appears in history and three kingdoms—Cola (Coromandel), Keraḷa (Malabar), and Pāṇḍya (southern tip of India)—are recorded as being in a state of continuous warfare. The people of the south, known as Tamils, were very different from the people of the north. Āryan ideas took time to penetrate, and the south was (and in many ways remains today) culturally distinct from the north.

During the early years of our era, many of the great Indian texts such as the *Mahābhārata* and the *Bhagavad-gītā* were compiled. Sanskrit became a living tongue. Buddhism evolved, and its doctrine underwent important changes. The plastic arts flowered, and new styles appeared. Politically, however, with the decline of Kushan power after the death of Kaniṣka, northern India broke up into petty kingdoms until, in AD 320, a new dynasty established itself in the old Magadha capital of Pāṭaliputra which was to revive the glory of the Maurya empire.

The first of the new kings took the name of the first Maurya, Chandragupta, and the new dynasty, to distinguish it from the earlier one, is known as the Guptas. Chandragupta's son, Samudragupta (c. 335–c. 375), extended his rule but was not successful against the Śakas. In about 388, however, during the reign of Chandragupta II (c. 375–415), the Śakas were defeated. Except for the north-west, the Gupta empire now covered all of northern India and the northern Deccan.

In the reign of Chandragupta II, early Indian civilisation probably reached its highest level. Later Indian legends refer to him as Vikramāditya

7 Statue of a Kushana king

('Sun of Heroism'), and the name was certainly one of Chandragupta's titles. Naturally, tradition has embroidered the glory of Chandragupta II, but in the works of the Chinese Buddhist traveller, Fa-hsien, we have at least some facts. Fa-hsien, unfortunately, was more interested in Buddhist temples and monasteries and collecting Buddhist legends than in reporting on social conditions, and nothing is said about Chandragupta himself, though Fa-hsien spent six years in his dominions. But he does mention that the country was peaceful and the administration non-repressive. Fa-hsien also records that most of the higher castes were vegetarian, and that only the lowest and the untouchables ate meat. Buddhism was still flourishing and its main effect on the old sacrificial religion had been to make it less harsh. From the point of view of ordinary people, the reign of Chandragupta II was probably the happiest period in the whole of India's history. During his reign Sanskrit literature reached a brilliant peak, particularly in the plays of Kālidāsa. The other arts also achieved a very high standard and it is from this period that a series of wall paintings can be dated in the caves of Ajantā, in the territory of vassal kings called Vākāṭakas.

Chandragupta II was succeeded by his son Kumāragupta (c. 415–454). In the last years of his reign India suffered another barbarian invasion, this time by the White Huns (Hūṇas)—possibly, though there is some doubt, a branch of the same people who were threatening the Roman empire in Europe at almost the same time. During the wars with the Huns, Kumāragupta died and Skandagupta (c. 455–467) ascended the throne. He managed to repel the invaders and bring a period of peace. After his death, the Gupta empire declined and local governors set themselves up as independent kings.

The next series of Hun invasions found no strong man to resist them. Towards the end of the fifth century, the north-west suffered a reign of terror. Buddhist monasteries (and universities) were destroyed, and monks were persecuted. Two of the Hun kings, Toramāṇa and his son Mihirakula, are remembered as oppressors of Buddhism. The latter's cruelty became legendary, but he appears to have been driven back by the Gupta ruler, Bālāditya, and in about AD 530 was defeated by Yaśodharman, king of Mandasor. After this, the Huns never seriously threatened India again.

They had, however, succeeded in destroying the Gupta empire which, by 550, had ceased to exist. A dynasty probably unrelated to the great Guptas ruled in Magadha until the eighth century. North of the Ganges, another kingdom, that of the Maukharis, with its capital at modern Kanauj, came into prominence; so, too, did a kingdom centred on modern Thanesar, in the watershed between the Sutlej and Jumna rivers. There, a king named Prabhākaravardhana—related to the Guptas of Magadha and the Maukhari king—had extended his rule among the remnants of the Huns in the Punjab. After his death, war broke out between the Guptas and the Maukharis, with the new Thanesar king supporting the Guptas. But both he and the Maukhari king were killed

8 Signature of Harṣa, from
a copperplate inscription

and, as the latter died without an heir, the two kingdoms were combined under Harṣa, the second son of Prabhākaravardhana.

Harṣa (606–647) ascended the throne at the age of sixteen and, during his reign, partly revived the splendour of the Gupta empire. We know a great deal about him, compared with his predecessors. His court poet, Bāṇa, compiled an account of Harṣa's rise to power, and for the last part of his reign there is the very full and observant description of the Chinese pilgrim, Hsüan Tsang, who was given a place at his court. Harṣa did not attempt to re-create the old Gupta central authority. His empire was feudal in structure and he kept control by constantly touring his dominions. But he was unable to regain the peace and security of the times of Chandragupta II, and the robbers and pirates whom Fa-hsien had then noted as being conspicuously absent, were active. Similarly, though Harṣa's state was extremely powerful, he was unable to expand into the Deccan.

In Hsüan Tsang's picture, Harṣa emerges as a tolerant and generous ruler, a lover of pomp who travelled with a vast retinue but would hear the complaint of an ordinary man from a small pavilion erected by the roadside. Foreign pilgrims came to visit the holy places of Buddhism and to attend the revived universities. There was great commercial activity.

Harṣa's reign was a brief rebirth of imperial grandeur. Literature and the arts were actively patronised. Harṣa himself was the author of a number of plays and Buddhist hymns. Though he supported Buddhism, at least in the latter part of his reign, the faith was in decline. New Hindu cults were coming into being and such practices as sati—widow-burning—were growing. On Harṣa's death without an heir the empire fell to pieces, never to be re-created by a Hindu king.

2 The Framework of Living

The early Indians saw their country as separated from the rest of the world by the great mountain range of the Himālayas. These immense snow-covered peaks play a special role in the imagery of Indian thought. Some historians have seen the Himālayas as a physical barrier isolating India from the rest of the world and, as such, an important factor in the development of a unique civilisation. This view has often been exaggerated. The Himālayas were never an impassable obstacle either to men or to ideas. Through the passes that cut the mountains which form a westward extension of the Himālayas came all the great invasions, from the Āryans to the Muslim conquerors. The Himālayas are the source of the two great river systems of northern India, which create between them fertile areas in which sophisticated cultures reached fruition. The source of one of these systems, the river Indus, which now runs mainly through Pakistan, gave its name to India—Sanskrit, *Sindhu*; Persian, *Hindu*; Greek, Ἰνδική Latin *India*. The five great tributaries of the Indus—the Jhelum, Chenāb, Rāvī, Beās, and Sutlej—watered an area now known as the Punjab (i.e. 'Five Rivers'), in which the pre-Āryan Indus civilisation reached a very high level over 2000 years before Christ.

Divided from the Indus basin by a desert and hills is a great plain watered by the river Ganges and its tributary the Jumna. The area between the two great rivers, stretching from around present-day Delhi in the west to Patna in the east, was called *Āryāvarta*, the home of the Āryans. It was a highly fertile land and, because of this, the goal of invaders. At the mouths of the Ganges on the Bay of Bengal, the river is joined by the Brahmaputra which has its source in Tibet.

To the south of *Āryāvarta* steadily rising land leads to another mountain mass, that of the Vindhyas. These mountains and their offshoots are sandstone ranges rising to about 3000 feet and were once covered with dense jungle through which the Āryan peoples found it difficult to pass. Beyond the mountains lay the Deccan (literally, 'The South'), bounded on either side by ranges of hills—the Western and Eastern Ghats (or

9 The Himālayas

'stairs'). The western range is a mountain wall running parallel to the shores of the Arabian Sea for about 600 miles. The numerous flat-topped peaks were used as fortresses throughout much of India's history. To the south the hills are pierced by a twenty-mile gap which joins the Malabar coast to the plains of the Karnatik. On the eastern side the hills are not so steep or continuous. Both ranges end in the Nīlgiri or 'Blue Mountains'.

The principal rivers of the south, except for two (the Tāptī and the Narbadā), flow eastwards into the Bay of Bengal. A tributary of one of these (the Tungabhadra) separates the Deccan from a large plain, the Tamil country, which evolved a culture distinctly its own and one which, despite the passage of time, remains distinct today. The peoples of south India, known as Dravidian, still speak different languages from those of the north and are of different racial origins. The peoples of the Indus civilisation destroyed by the Āryan invaders about the second millennium BC seem to have been racially a mixture of the Mediterranean type found all over the Middle East and of the Proto-Australoid, related to the aborigines of Australia. In south India today the people are usually a blend of these two racial elements.

From north to south, India is nearly 2000 miles in length. Because of this, there are wide variations in climate between various parts of the country. In the north, along the Himālayas, winters are cold and frosty with occasional falls of snow, while the plains of northern India have winters in which the days are cool and the nights often very cold. In the north, however, the hot weather is extremely hot. In the Deccan, the difference in the seasons is not so great. The Tamil plain is always hot, but the temperature never reaches the gruelling level it does in the north.

Life in India has always revolved around the coming of 'the rains'—the monsoon which brings the water so essential to the growing of crops. Generally speaking, rain is rare between October and May, and during this period crops can only be grown with the artificial aid of irrigation. Towards the end of the period, there is a slow intensification of heat until, around the end of April, the temperature in the northern plains moves well past 100 °F. with dry, hot winds. The earth begins to crack, animals die of thirst, and men seek the shade.

Towards the end of June the rains fall in great downpours, making the land, almost overnight, green and alive. The monsoon lasts for about two months and then the rains slowly die away. India is a land of extremes, and even the life-giving rains can bring death. Rivers, swollen to many times their normal size, flood vast areas of land and there is often plague to intensify the destruction. But to Indians the monsoon has always been welcome and its coming a time of thanksgiving to the gods.

10 A sacred island in the river Brahmaputra

RELIGION AND SOCIETY

All Men are Born Unequal

In no other civilisation has religion played such an intimate role in every aspect of the social structure as it did, and to a large extent still does, in India. At the foundation of Indian society is the unalterable concept of the inequality of man. There is a hierarchy of classes, each separate in its duties, each with a special way of life.

A man's position in society was the consequence of *karma* (see p. 6) whose operation conformed to a universal or sacred law, that of *dharma*. This law in human society regulated all things, all behaviour, and could not be escaped. Once born into a particular class, a man was kept there by *karma* which forced him to carry out the particular functions and obligations of that class. There was no escape except through death and rebirth. Originally the Āryans had produced this 'divine' order of society with purely racist intentions. Later, of course, it became the support of the

23

upper classes. There were protests against it—Buddhism being the most powerful and, within limitations, the most successful—but, because such an order did support the existence of privileged classes, it resisted and survived.

The Four Classes

At the end of the Rig-Vedic period, the division of society into four classes came to be regarded as divinely fixed. In theory, at least, all Āryans belong to one of the four, except for children, ascetics, and widows. Others outside the system, usually the conquered peoples, did not in effect have any social status at all. Admittedly they existed, but they could not take part in the religious life of the community. The three upper classes, brāhman, kṣatriya, and vaiśya, were also divided from the lowest, the śūdra, which, unlike the others, did not have an initiation ceremony. The duties of the classes were precisely laid down. The brāhman should spend his time in studying and teaching, in making the sacrifices and in receiving and giving gifts; the kṣatriya should protect the people, study, and sacrifice; the vaiśya, though he should also sacrifice and study, should make his main purposes the breeding of cattle, agriculture, trading, and money-lending. The śūdra's only duty was to serve the other three.

Naturally, real life rarely if ever fitted the ideal of the lawmakers. The brāhmans who wrote the laws were optimists and their world was a philosopher's Utopia. In practice, the rules of conduct for each class were frequently ignored and very often broken.

According to the brāhman, he was able to destroy rulers and armies if they tried to take away his privileges, because he possessed magical powers. He demanded precedence and respect above all others. Even amongst these exalted people there were many divisions. Some brāhmans were learned scholars, others, in the villages, hardly better than fortune-tellers. Though the brāhman was of the priestly class, by no means all brāhmans were priests—primarily because there are limits on how many priests a community actually needs. Some spent their time in hermitages, living a truly religious life among the wild things of the forest. Others lived in colonies supported by gifts from rulers and ordinary people. Others, still, were employed by kings and some became the founders of dynasties themselves. Though various trades—including agriculture—were in theory barred to brāhmans, in practice they could be found pursuing most activities, even that of professional spy. But in whatever profession he

11 Two brāhmans (*bottom left*) seated before the king

chose, a brāhman could not be tortured or sentenced to death, nor was he liable for the payment of taxes. However, though there was no clear ruling on whether a brāhman engaged in a secular profession was entitled to the same respect as a practising priest, it seems that special rights were indeed only granted to those who lived by carrying out sacrifices and by teaching.

Brāhmanic privileges, of course, inspired jealousy, and there have survived a number of satirical attacks on brāhmans who did not live up to their responsibilities. But there are very few direct attacks even in the Buddhist texts. Again, in practice, it is highly probable that the pretensions of the brāhmans were often ignored, depending, no doubt, upon the degree of fear felt towards them and their possibly magical powers.

The kṣatriya, as 'protector of the people', was the ruler, the fighter of battles or preserver of peace. There seems to have been considerable conflict at one time between brāhmans and kṣatriyas over which took precedence, but certainly by Maurya times (the beginning of the period covered by this book) the brāhman was theoretically first—although his position depended upon the attitude and power of the kṣatriya involved. Though the kṣatriyas formed the military class, not all kṣatriyas were soldiers and there are records of kṣatriya merchants and craftsmen. All kṣatriyas, however, were supposed to have a military education. An example of the Indian ability to absorb foreign elements into the system can be seen here; new conquerors were said to be kṣatriyas who had 'lapsed' and who could return to the fold by making a number of specially prescribed sacrifices. Among the privileges claimed by all kṣatriyas—even those who had gone into trade—were two forms of marriage. One of these was marriage by capture, and the other one in which a girl chose her own husband from an assembly of suitors.

Though, like the brāhman and the kṣatriya, the vaiśya was permitted to learn the sacred texts and to go through a ceremony of initiation, he was considered very much their inferior. Originally the vaiśyas had been agriculturists, presumably the reason for their humble status. But their position had improved considerably. Many were wealthy merchants and were organised into powerful guilds. It was mainly from this class that Buddhism and Jainism received support and, during the rule of the great Buddhist kings, the vaiśyas formed a genuine bourgeoisie. According to surviving records, they exercised considerable influence on the state and many of them were great patrons of art and learning. Nevertheless, discrimination still existed; vaiśyas usually submitted to being more heavily taxed than others, thus, in effect, acknowledging their continuing inferior status in relation to the two higher classes.

The position of the śūdra was very much that of a second-class citizen.

Even persons whose class origin was high but who were of illegitimate birth were classed as śūdras. Generally speaking, anybody who was not 'respectable' was automatically a śūdra and this logic applied to those who refused to accept the new brāhman orthodoxies and preferred to stick to the old ways. There were two kinds of śūdras, 'pure' and 'impure', a division dictated by custom and profession. The 'impure' were virtually the same as untouchables. Śūdras had very few rights and a great many duties. As only past evil deeds could (according to the theory of karma) have made them śūdras in the first place, they had to work hard to amass sufficient good deeds in this life to justify a better position in the next.

According to brāhmanical texts, the śūdra should eat the remains of his master's food and wear his discarded clothes. A brāhman who killed a śūdra merely performed the same penance as he would have done for killing a cat or a dog. The śūdra was no more than a servant with little hope of a better life—but again, in practice, things were different. Śūdras are reported as having become merchants. There were even śūdra kings. Though śūdras were not permitted to know or even to hear the most sacred texts, others were open to them. As workers, they were given some protection by the law, and employers were compelled to make contracts with them specifying the obligations of both parties. Śūdras, however, were obliged to give the state free labour on one or two days a month.

Untouchables

Below the śūdras existed groups of people who carried out various necessary but unpleasant tasks. Some of them were probably aboriginal tribes conquered by the Āryans. The most important of the groups was known as *caṇḍāla*. Caṇḍālas were not allowed to live in Āryan towns and villages, and their main task, in theory anyway, was to dispose of and burn the dead as well as act as executioners. By Gupta times contact with them was assumed to be so polluting to the other classes that they had to announce their presence by sounding a wooden clapper. A man of the higher classes would bathe his eyes with perfumed water if he were unfortunate enough to catch sight of a caṇḍāla, and he would be defiled if even the shadow of an outcaste fell between him and the sun.

Certain 'unclean' trades were reserved to the untouchables—the tanning of leather, for example, because this involved the killing of an animal. But they also included such trades as that of the basket-maker and builder of chariots, for which there is no similar explanation. The untouchable could not enter a temple. (Only since India became independent in 1947 has this discrimination been prohibited by law.)

Foreigners were automatically untouchable, but were not subject to the same oppressive discrimination. They were known as *mlecchas*. They could, however, take no part in the social order. A mleccha might, if he stayed long enough, be absorbed into one of the classes, even the higher ones. Ascetics, because they had renounced society, were also technically outsiders, but were treated with great respect. It also seems likely, from the repeated warnings that can be found in texts against allowing untouchables to grow too powerful, that some had actually reached positions of influence.

Mixed Marriages

Strictly speaking there should have been no intermarriage between members of the four classes but, because human nature is universally and eternally contradictory, such marriages did take place in early India. The lawmakers sensibly adapted the law to suit the circumstances. Nevertheless, it was virtually impossible to be accepted into a higher class through marriage, though it was very easy, for a wide variety of reasons, to fall into a lower one. In theory, if a man did not accept the responsibilities of his class, then the punishment was impurity or outcasting, either temporary or permanent. There is plenty of evidence, however, that in the more sophisticated urban communities penances were ignored. It was the ruler who was supposed to maintain the purity of the classes, and some attempted to do so. But interclass marriage was in fact, and within limitations, permitted. A man of a high class could marry a woman of a lower one, but not the other way round. The children of a marriage of the first type occupied a position between that of their father and their mother. Offspring of the second type, however, were of a lower status than that of either parent. As with everything else in India, there were exceptions to this, too, including a class of charioteers and bards.

Caste

When the Portuguese settled in India in the sixteenth century, they discovered that the Hindu community was divided into a large number of groups. These the Portuguese called *castas* which means tribes, clans, or

12 A *mleccha* or foreigner (*left*), and an outcaste, mounted on winged lions

families. The word has come to be used to define the basic Hindu social groups. It is, however, a confusing misuse of the word. Today there are about 3000 castes—but there are still only four classes. Caste is a system of groups within the class and is of comparatively recent origin. The Indian word for such groups is *jāti*. It is only infrequently used in early Indian literature and even then it does not mean what it means today, i.e. an exclusive group which normally permits marriage only within the group (endogamy), allows food only to be received from and eaten with members of the same or higher group (commensality), and whose members follow a group trade or profession (craft-exclusiveness).

The development of caste took place over a very long period of time and there is no real certainty about its origin. The most plausible explanation lies in trade-guilds, and there is plenty of evidence of whole villages following one trade and of special quarters reserved for them in towns. As late as the seventh century AD, the Chinese traveller Hsüan Tsang (see p. 19)—though observing the four classes and mentioning many mixed ones—does not give us any clue as to whether caste in the modern sense existed in his time. By the Middle Ages, when the Hindu social system became more or less rigid, there is no doubt that caste was fully established.

Slavery

It is possible that the institution of slavery in early India originated in the position assigned by the Āryans to the people they conquered. Certainly the word given to them, *dāsa*, in later times came to mean a slave. According to the *Mahābhārata*, prisoners captured in war became the victor's slaves until they were ransomed. Slavery was perpetuated by making the children of slaves into slaves of their parents' masters. A man could sell himself and his family into slavery or be made a slave as a punishment for some crime or for debt. In the latter case, the slave had to be freed when he had paid with his labour the amount of the debt.

Slaves played no important role in Indian economic life and were normally employed as house servants. They could be bought and sold, but their well-being was protected by law. The *Arthaśāstra* displays a remarkably liberal approach to the institution of slavery. Children could not be sold as slaves except in times of severe distress. Slaves could own and inherit property. Slave-girls were protected from the lust of their master. A slave-girl raped had to be set free and paid compensation. Generally speaking, it would appear that slaves were much better treated in India than in other slave-owning societies, though there are references in some texts which might be taken to indicate that, on occasion, slaves rebelled.

In the king's palace slave-women often formed an Amazon guard to protect the ruler's harem. There was also a substantial trade in girls for the harem itself, many of them from Greece. Indian girls seem to have found a ready market in the Roman empire.

Family

The Indian family was (and to some extent still is) what is known as 'joint'—i.e. brothers, uncles, nephews, and cousins often lived under the same roof and owned the family home in common. In early India, the family might include adopted children and, if it was not poor, there would also be a large number of servants. As men were entitled to have more than one wife, the group was often very large. The family was the basic unit of the social system and population was not assessed in terms of individuals but in families.

The family was bound together by the rite of commemorating ancestors (*śrāddha*), which linked the dead and the living, giving the family a deep

30

13 An Amazon guard

sense of continuity and solidarity. A member of a family was always sure of some sort of help from his relations as a matter of right and of duty. The head of the family did not have an entirely free hand, for his power was limited by the Sacred Law and by custom and he was probably considered less as the absolute owner of family property than as a sort of trustee. The law books are somewhat at odds about the rights of the father over his children. One says that he could sell them, another expressly forbids it.

The Law also provided for breaking up the family when it became too large. Normally this would happen on the death of the head, when the property was divided amongst his sons; the eldest son had no special privilege on this occasion. The family might also be divided if the father became an ascetic or, under certain circumstances, if he were old or incurably ill. The law books give highly detailed instructions for the division of property; although they vary from book to book, most—but not all—agree that women had no right of inheritance. Over the centuries, joint family property ceased to include individual personal possessions; this does not, however, appear to have been the case during the period covered by this book.

The Four Stages

As Āryan society was divided into four classes, so the Āryan's personal life was divided into four stages (*āśrama*). The first was *brahmacārin*, when he

31

was invested with the sacred thread. At this point, childhood ended and the youth became a student. The second stage was *gṛhastha* when, having mastered the Vedas, he married and became a householder; the third was *vānaprastha*, when having seen his grandchildren and assured himself that his line was established, he left to become a hermit; and lastly came *sanyyāsin*, when he left his hermitage, after freeing his soul by meditation and penance from the bonds of the material world, and became a homeless wanderer.

Naturally, this order of things was an ideal. Some Āryans never completed the first stage in the manner laid down. Others became hermits without going through the stage of being a householder, and so on. But the order remained an ideal that many attempted to follow. As the first stage of life began with the initiation ceremony, the child was not, before that time, really a member of the Āryan community. This did not mean that his life before receiving the sacred thread was not adequately surrounded by religious rites. On the contrary, such rites began before birth and continued for the rest of his life.

Childhood

Initially, three rites were performed by a child's parents-to-be—to make conception sure, to produce a male child, and to see that the child was protected inside the womb. At birth itself a ceremony took place before the cutting of the umbilical cord. A number of spells were whispered into the baby's ear, honey and ghee (clarified butter) were put in its mouth, and it was given a name which was kept secret until the initiation ceremony was performed some years later. For ten days after the child's birth both parents were ritually impure. On the tenth day the child was given a public name and the parents' period of impurity was at an end.

As in most early societies, food played an important part in ritual. When the child was six months old, he was given a mouthful of meat, fish and rice mixed with curds, honey, and ghee. Verses from the Vedas were recited and ghee was poured on a fire. At three years of age, if the child was male, his hair was shaved off, leaving only a topknot. There were other minor ceremonies to do with such things as the piercing of the ears or first learning of the alphabet. It seems highly unlikely that, except in particularly pious families, all these ceremonies *were* performed, but they do indicate the importance of children and especially of male children in the life of the family. At least one son was needed to carry out his father's funeral rites—without which passage to the next world would be difficult. The overwhelming desire for male children felt even to the present day by Hindu parents stems from this. Girls were of no use, because they could not carry out the death ceremonies nor perpetuate the line; on marriage they became members of their husband's family. To reinforce this religious distaste for girl children, there was also the secular necessity of having to find dowries for them. For these two very sound reasons girl children were not wanted.

From the literature of the time, it appears that children—even girls—were given considerable freedom. In poetry they are usually depicted with great sentimentality. But the freedom of childhood soon came to an end. The children of the poor were set to work. For those of the higher classes, there were lessons, usually under a family tutor. These lessons included reading and arithmetic but it was not until the initiation ceremony that the boy began to learn the Vedas. Though the education of girls was not considered of importance, they, too, were often taught with the boys until the time of the latters' initiation.

The Sacred Thread

The ceremony of initiation, of the 'second birth' (*upanayana*), was the privilege only of the first three classes—brāhman, kṣatriya, and vaiśya. The śūdra and all others were excluded and were not allowed to hear or learn the most sacred texts. For the three higher classes, the most suitable age for initiation into class and society differed; it was eight years old for the brāhman, eleven for the kṣatriya, and twelve for the vaiśya, though these ages were not necessarily strictly kept to. The rite itself was very old, going back to the time before the Āryans entered India. The most important part was the investing of the boy, dressed as an ascetic and holding a staff in his hand, with the sacred thread (*yajñopavīta*), a cord which was placed over his right shoulder and under his left arm. This he was supposed to wear continuously. The cord was made up of three threads, each of nine twisted strands, made of cotton for brāhmans, hemp for kṣatriyas, and wool for vaiśyas.

During the ceremony, a verse (called the Gāyatrī) from the *Rig-Veda* was whispered into the ear of the boy by the officiating priest. The verse

33

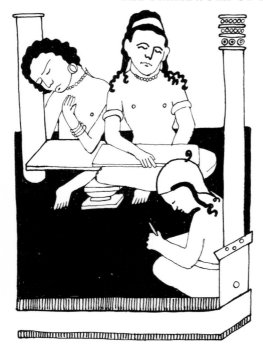

14 Children learning the
sacred texts

can only be spoken by the first three classes and is considered the most holy
passage in that most holy of scriptures.

> Let us think on the lovely splendour of the god Savitri [the sun god]
> that he may improve our minds.

It seems probable that, at some time before the beginning of the present
era, at least some kṣatriyas and vaiśyas had abandoned the ceremony in its
complete form, as the use of the phrase 'twice-born' became another way
of describing a brāhman. After the ceremony, the boy became a student
with several years to go before he moved into the next stage of life, that
of the householder.

The Years of Learning

The student's education was supposed to take place in the home of his
teacher (*guru*). There he first learned the devotions for morning, midday,
and evening. His main subject for study was the Vedas, and there were

various methods to help him commit the many thousands of verses to memory. Then there were the 'limbs of the Veda', subsidiary knowledge necessary to the correct understanding of the sacred texts. These consisted of how to perform sacrifice; the correct pronunciation of words; metre and prosody; the interpretation of obscure words; grammar; and the science of the calendar. There might also be lessons in metaphysics of which, like the six 'limbs', there were six schools. The Sacred Law might be explained, and sometimes secular subjects such as mathematics, astronomy, and literature. The kind of education a student received depended very much upon the qualifications and the inclinations of his particular guru.

Though, ideally, all young men of the upper classes should have received such an education, it is highly unlikely that many actually did. Not unnaturally, those of the warrior-class had more emphasis placed upon military training and on government, while vaiśyas learned a trade. So, too, the ideal of a small number of pupils with a single guru was not always achieved. There were a number of universities in which some classes were said to have as many as 500 students. Frequently, too, the students did not live in their teacher's house.

For Buddhists and Jains, education centred around the monasteries and some of these acquired a tremendous reputation. Perhaps the most famous, founded in Gupta times, was that at Nālandā in present-day Bihar, of which Hsüan Tsang gives a description. According to this Chinese traveller, the Vedas, Hindu philosophy, logic, grammar, and medicine, as well as Buddhist studies, were taught to a student body of 10,000. The idea of monastic schools was later taken up by the Hindus.

Marriage

Student life was supposed to last twelve years. In his early twenties, a young man would return home to the normal life of his class. On leaving his teacher he made a gift, its size depending upon the wealth of his family. After a ritual bath, he was free to dress, wear jewelry, and eat the food of his class. Now he was expected to marry as soon as possible; by doing so, he helped—through the performance of the household sacrifices —to promote religion; by having children, he assured his father of a good afterlife; and enjoyed sexual pleasure. These were the three main purposes of marriage.

For the parents, their son's marriage presented many problems. Horoscopes had to be cast, relationships carefully established, for marriage was not permitted between persons with a common paternal ancestor within seven generations or a maternal one within five (though this was not followed in the south). Ideally, the age of the bride was supposed to be one-third of that of the groom. He was to be at least twenty. Early medical texts stated that the strongest, and therefore the best children, were borne by mothers over sixteen, but child marriages did take place in early times, and became common after the Middle Ages.

The marriage ceremony differs little today from that laid down in the *Rig-Veda*. The family of the bride paid all the expenses and also had to supply a dowry. A marriage was—and still is—a very costly affair. It was also ritually complicated. The bridegroom, richly dressed and accompanied by relatives and friends, went to the house of the bride where he received from her father a drink of curds and honey. In the courtyard of the house, a pavilion had been erected and the bride and groom entered separately and sat down on either side of a curtain. The brāhman priest muttered sacred verses and the curtain was taken away, so allowing the couple to see each other, very often for the first time. The bride's father then formally gave his daughter to the groom and received in return a promise always to behave well to her in terms of three traditional aims of life—piety, wealth, and pleasure. Offerings of ghee and rice were then thrown on to the sacred fire and the groom grasped the bride's right hand and knotted a corner of his robe to one of hers. Treading on a millstone, they walked seven steps together, the bride placing her feet on a small heap of rice at each step. A sprinkling of holy water, and the principal ceremony was over. At various times and in various places, the ceremony might differ in detail, but not in the many sacred verses which had to be chanted.

After the main part of the ceremony, the couple went to the bridegroom's house where a sacrifice to the domestic fire was performed. In the evening, both gazed at the Pole Star, a symbol of faithfulness. For three nights, the couple slept side by side; during this time they were supposed not to have intercourse. On the fourth night, however, the husband performed a rite to encourage conception and the marriage was consummated.

The length of the ceremony and the many magical verses which had to be pronounced and sacrifices which had to be performed indicate the importance of marriage in the ideal society envisaged by the early lawmakers. But the ceremony described, though it remains the usual one today, was not the only one in use in early India. A marriage could even take place without any ceremony; such a marriage was held just as valid as the other. In fact, there were eight types of marriage. Four of them were considered perfectly respectable, even for brāhmans. The first was as described above, the second was when a father gave his daughter to a priest in payment of at least part of the fee for performing a sacrifice. The third was one in which no dowry was paid beyond a token one in the form of a cow or a bull. And the fourth was one in which there was neither dowry nor token. The remaining four were considered, at least by the orthodox, with disfavour. These consisted of marriage by the consent of both parties, in which there was no ceremony other than a simple declaration; marriage by purchase; marriage by capture; and marriage, if it could be called such, by the seduction of a girl while she was asleep, mentally deranged, or drunk.

Marriage by consent, known as *gāndharva*, was frequently only temporary, but generally speaking was not thought particularly dishonourable. Such marriages were the subject of a vast number of highly romantic tales. The last three forms of marriage, however, were given the names of demons and regarded as a reluctant concession to the evil of man. The last of all was particularly objectionable, and only for the very lowest in the social scale. Nevertheless, the existence of these forms of marriage at least showed that the law-makers did not live entirely in the clouds. There was also provision for legitimising the last four by means of religious ceremonies. A further type, a variant of gāndharva, also seems to have existed. This permitted a girl who was not married off in the usual way soon after reaching puberty, to choose her own bridegroom. There are a number of references to this form in epic literature.

Once the marriage ceremony was over, the man had reached the state of householder. It was now his duty to devote himself to the three traditional aims of life as he had promised his bride's father. That of pleasure needs no explanation, nor does that of wealth. But piety—gaining merit by following the Sacred Law—involved a number of religious duties. Apart from the ceremonies of birth, marriage, and death there were the daily observance of the 'Five Great Sacrifices' (*pañca-mahāyajña*). There was the sacrifice to Brahman, the World-Spirit, by reciting the Vedas; there was the worship of ancestors, by libations of water; the worship of the gods, by the pouring of ghee on the sacred fire; the worship of all

37

15 The five heroes of the *Mahābhārata* and their communal wife, Draupadi

living things, by the scattering of food for animals, birds, and spirits on
the threshold of the house; and the worship of men, by hospitality. For an
orthodox household these sacrifices were to be carried out three times a
day, at sunrise, midday, and sunset.

Divorce and Polygamy

A marriage duly sanctified by the correct ceremonial was supposed to be
unbreakable. According to the *Laws of Manu*, a wife who committed
adultery with a man of higher caste could be reinstated after a period of
penance, but if she committed adultery with someone of lower caste she
was to be torn to pieces by dogs. But again, the *secular* law books were
conscious of the real world. The *Arthaśāstra* permitted divorce by mutual
consent or if one partner was in fear of the other. This only applied to
a marriage that had not been solemnised by religious rites, but desertion
was ground for divorce even in the case of a religious marriage, the period
varying between one and twenty years according to circumstances and
class. By Gupta times, however, divorce was almost completely prohibited
for the upper classes. Though a man's possession of more than one wife
was generally frowned upon by both the sacred and secular law books, it
was apparently fashionable with those classes who could afford the
expense. Kings almost always kept a number of wives. The reverse of
polygamy, polyandry, was not thought respectable, though in the great

epic of the *Mahābhārata* the five heroes shared one wife, a situation which has not been adequately explained away, even by much learned commentary. Polyandry was a common practice amongst certain tribes (it still is amongst some in the Himālaya region) and amongst the lower orders.

Old Age and Death

A man of orthodox faith who rigidly followed the Sacred Law was expected to become a hermit after his sons had had sons. He could either leave his wife to the care of her children or take her with him. In the hermitage, by performing rites and studying, he would raise himself above the things of the world. When that stage had been achieved—and with nothing but a begging bowl, a staff, and a piece of cloth to put about his loins—he would leave the hermitage and became a wanderer until death. Of course, this stage of life was not for everybody, but a considerable number did follow the Sacred Law. It is not entirely unusual even today.

Indians were no exception to the belief common amongst ancient peoples that contact with a corpse was to be avoided. Such contact was left to the outcastes, whose job it was to prepare and carry the corpse to the cremation grounds. This was done as soon after death as possible. The corpse was carried on a litter with the mourners following, led by the eldest. As the body was being cremated, they circled the pyre in an anti-clockwise direction, while sacred texts were intoned. Then the mourners bathed in a near-by pond or river and returned home, led this time by the youngest. Three days after the cremation the charred bones were gathered together and thrown into a river—if possible into that most sacred of rivers, the Ganges.

For ten days after the cremation, libations of water and offerings of bowls of rice and milk were made for the soul which was, during this period, in a kind of limbo and might do harm to the relatives. After the last rite, the soul acquired a form-without-substance in which to pursue its journey, nourished by the ancestor-worship of the family.

16 A brāhman begging for food. Over his shoulder is the sacred thread

39

For the higher classes, the funeral ceremony and its attendant rites remain unchanged today.

Not every family in early India burned its dead. In some cases, there were good economic reasons for this, especially among the lower classes: and in arid country there was an absence of trees to supply wood for the pyre. If literary references are anything to go by (and they are frequently the only sources available), some of the peoples of early India left the bodies of the dead to be eaten by wild animals and birds.

The Position of Women

According to most of the early texts, woman always occupied a subordinate position—to her parents when she was a child, to her husband when a wife, and to her children when a widow. Women did, however, within certain limitations, have personal property rights and when a woman died her possessions passed to her daughters. Women could take up a religious life and, until the present era, were allowed access to Vedic knowledge, though this was prohibited later. The Buddhists even made a place for women as nuns. But the real function of women in Indian society was to marry and have children. This did not prevent women of the higher classes from having an education, and there are surviving fragments of poetry and plays by women authors.

In early India, there does not appear to have been anything like the seclusion of women which became common after the Muslim invasions. Nevertheless, the king's harem was closely guarded and the women were not allowed any freedom. Women of the upper classes, if not actually secluded, were kept away from the opposite sex. The *Arthaśāstra* details a series of fines for what it calls immodest behaviour. In early Indian literature, both sacred and secular, there is often a dual attitude towards women. There are many praises for the loving wife, abundant and faithful, who is not just a chattel but 'half the man'. She was to be treated with love and certainly never beaten. On the other hand, women were said to be naturally lustful and, unless constantly watched, would be promiscuous or, failing the opportunity, lesbian. Fortunately, even in early India, everyday life was not always what the law-givers and the philosophers believed it to be.

If, according to the texts, a wife's position was one of honour surrounded by suspicion, that of a widow, at least in an orthodox family,

17 Concubines

was very hard. There is no doubt that in very early times widows could and did remarry, but the practice slowly died out among the upper classes. After her husband's death a woman was condemned to only one meal a day, without meat, wine, salt, or honey. She could wear no jewelry, or coloured clothes. Her time, spent in prayer, was considered to be a waiting period; when she died, she might in the afterlife be reunited with her husband. If she behaved badly, it was not only her own soul that was in danger; so, too, was that of her dead husband. Consequently, a widow's family kept constant watch to ensure that she did not stray from her ascetic life. She was not allowed to attend family festivals, and her existence was acutely miserable. It is hardly surprising that a woman often burned herself to death on the pyre of her dead husband. The practice, known as *sati* (suttee)—a word which means 'virtuous' and refers to the woman, not to the act itself—is of very early origin but was not common until around the fifth or sixth century A D.

Sexual Life

Of the three aims of life (see p. 36), pleasure, though the least important, had a special place in the Indian division of activity. Of all the permissible pleasures, that of sexual relations was considered the best. It was, for man and wife, a religious duty, and the husband was supposed to have intercourse with his wife not later than eight days after the end of every period of menstruation. Sexual relations were considered as an art, and one of some refinement. There were numerous works containing detailed instructions, as well as formulae for the preparation of aphrodisiacs. The most famous of these works is the *Kāmasūtra*, allegedly compiled by Vātsyāyana and written some time during the first five centuries of this era. It is a handbook for the sophisticated town-dweller, a little pedantic and not particularly erotic, but containing some extremely wise advice for newly married husbands. Homosexuality, though not unknown in early India, received very little attention in the literature of the times.

For sexual life outside marriage, brothels existed. They were very carefully supervised by the state, but their use was mainly confined to the lower classes. Men of superior class were more interested in courtesans. The courtesan was not subject to any of the restrictions which bound ordinary women. In a real sense, she was outside the religious organisation of society, though very much a part of the secular one. Some occupied positions of great honour and authority. There was, however, one class of prostitute with at least some sort of religious sanction. These were the temple prostitutes, or *devadāsī*. Though there is a reference to them in an inscription written soon after the death of Aśoka, such prostitutes were probably rare until mediaeval times.

THE STATE

Early Indians, unlike the Greeks, were not interested in political philosophy, in arguing about the nature and origin of the state, or in theorising about ideal situations of law and government. They were, however, very interested in the actual mechanics of ruling, in the practical organisation of the state. A number of texts on this subject have survived. They do not necessarily describe how an actual system worked, but only how it ought to work. Some historians have accepted these texts so uncritically as to give a false impression of early Indian statecraft. All of the texts contain elements of the truth and are therefore extremely valuable. But it is a good thing to remember that, generally speaking, Indian kings—like other kings in other countries—were severely practical people and not much given to discussing the finer points of the business of government. They left such matters to the writers of texts.

The King

In early India, the king was a symbol of the state, ruling with divine sanction and consecrated with divine power which was periodically renewed throughout his reign by a series of rites. A state without a king was virtually unthinkable, though among certain tribes something like a republic was not unknown. However, the periods of anarchy which shook India between the time of the Mauryas and that of the Guptas convinced many Indian thinkers that the trouble was due to an absence of kings. Of course they were right, for where there is no strong ruler anarchy prevails. The propaganda of such thinkers—the *Rāmāyaṇa* is an example—was designed to enhance the prestige of kingship in the popular mind. It was during these uneasy years, when many people thought that the world was about to come to an end, that legends about the divine origins of kingship were composed to buttress the position of the ruler. Naturally, such legends had the wholehearted support of kings themselves. But it should be remembered that divinity is unusually commonplace in India. In one sense or another the gods are everywhere, even in stones. Furthermore, the Indian gods are neither infallible nor incapable of sin.

Kings were undoubtedly treated with great respect but, at least in the view of the upper classes, that respect was not solely derived from their divinity. Buddhists and Jains, in fact, rejected the king's divine pretensions, and the king's divinity, even when accepted, was limited. His proper function was not to do what he liked but actively to protect the people. In early India, this meant more than just maintaining the physical security of the state. The king's overriding duty was to preserve the order of society as laid down by the sacred texts. If he chose to go his own way, then the brāhmans were supposed to remind him of his responsibilities. If their appeals were ignored, it was their duty to overthrow him. There are numerous stories of brāhmanic revolts, no doubt designed to remind kings of the probable consequences of flouting the Sacred Law. Undoubtedly, there were kings strong enough and wilful enough to go their own way, but the brāhman's 'right to rebel' on purely moral grounds must have acted as some check upon their activities.

All textbooks on statecraft advised the king to listen to his ministers and keep an ear open for public opinion. In very early times, popular assemblies exercised some control over the ruler but, over the years, these disappeared. There is evidence—unfortunately none of it historical—of kings being overthrown by popular rebellion. The *Rāmāyaṇa*, whose hero Rāma is the image of the ideal king, tells how he exiles his wife Sītā because his subjects expressed doubts about her chastity, even though he knows she is innocent of any immorality. Rāma does so because his first duty is to 'please the people'.

The king's duty to his subjects covered every aspect of the social and economic order. He protected caste and class by taking action against those who broke caste customs; the family, by punishing adultery and ensuring that the laws of inheritance were properly observed; the poor, by punishing extortion and oppression; and the rich, by suppressing robbers. Religion was supported by liberal grants to temples and priests. He protected the general welfare by developing irrigation, seeing that famine was relieved, and by keeping trade and commerce flourishing. The ideal king was one who spent most of his day on affairs of state. The *Arthaśāstra* suggests only four and a half hours' sleep and three hours for meals and recreation. It is not known whether many kings approached this ideal but it seems highly doubtful that there were more than a few.

Normally the king was succeeded by his eldest son, but there was nothing rigid about the order of succession. According to the Sacred Law, a diseased, maimed, or infirm prince was not to succeed. According to the *Arthaśāstra*, a wicked prince—even if he were the only son—should not be allowed to ascend the throne. There are examples of kings nominating their successors. The absence of any strict law of succession caused many disputes in the kingdoms of early India and in a number of cases undoubtedly led to their downfall. Intrigues among the king's relatives were often dangerous, and the textbooks warned the king to control his family and to employ spies to keep a sharp watch so that any conspiracy could be easily suppressed. If a king died without an heir, the principal figures in the kingdom—the courtiers, nobles, merchants, and religious leaders—would sometimes meet and choose a king. This was what happened in the case of Harṣa (see p. 19).

Administration

Practically all textbooks advised the king to appoint wise councillors and to listen to what they had to say. In practice, it obviously depended upon

18 A king receiving tribute

the personality of the king. Sometimes the king's council made decisions in his absence on tour or in battle, but the precise duties of the councillors are somewhat vague. There seems usually to have been one man who acted as chief councillor. With pious kings, the court priest exercised considerable influence. Obviously, the councillors responsible for the treasury and the collection of taxes were always important. In Gupta times, there was also a 'minister of peace and war', the equivalent of today's foreign minister, though he also had certain definite military functions and frequently accompanied the king on the battlefield.

In general, neither the king nor his council made laws in the modern sense. The decrees they issued were assumed to relate to specific applications of the Sacred Law and of custom. In practice, however, certain kings did make new laws. Aśoka is one example; but he was not an orthodox ruler. Royal decrees were prepared by a special body of secretaries, and great precautions were taken to see that the final drafts actually represented the king's views. A number of witnesses affixed their marks to guarantee the authenticity of each copy before it was released. Records were very carefully kept to ensure that there was no error.

In Maurya times, practically every aspect of activity was controlled by the state through a corps of superintendents. There were even officials who controlled liquor, gambling, and prostitution. Economic life was a direct state responsibility and a great deal of the country's economic activity was owned and operated by the state. There were large state farms, and factories for spinning and weaving. In some cases, the state might lease a mine or a pearl fishery to private operators and take a percentage of the profits.

Obviously, this close identification of the state with the economic life of the country called for a large civil service. Its members were paid salaries, some of them very large. To discourage corruption, appointments were often duplicated, possibly on the assumption that one official would keep an eye on the other.

After the end of Maurya times, officials were rewarded with grants of the revenue from a particular village or district instead of a salary. This method of payment was not entirely unknown in pre-Maurya times, but its expansion created a new class of privileged, semi-feudal chiefs who came between the king and the people and thus helped to weaken the hold of the central authority.

In Maurya and Gupta times, the provinces into which early Indian kingdoms were divided were usually governed by members of the royal family. Beneath the governors of provinces—and usually appointed by them—were the governors of districts. In Gupta times—and possibly before—these officials were advised and assisted by local councils probably consisting of important local personalities. Megasthenes reports that, in the time of Chandragupta Maurya, cities also had councils. The city governor was sometimes the military commander as well, and controlled local troops, police, and spies. The latter played an extremely important role in the administrative system.

The *Arthaśāstra* insisted that the government must keep a careful check on everybody. This was done through officials who were responsible for the supervision of forty households each. These officials controlled taxes, recorded births and deaths and the income and expenditure of the people under their care. They even noted the names of visitors. This information was kept in the form of permanent records. Open control was reinforced by the activities of secret agents. The *Arthaśāstra* gave detailed instructions for the organisation of espionage. Apart from more routine activities such as collecting information and passing it on to their superiors, the spies performed another essential function by keeping the king in touch with public opinion. They also acted as propagandists, spreading reports in praise of the ruler. Though it would appear that the Maurya empire had at least some of the characteristics of a modern police state, the overall picture is not one of fear and oppression.

The smallest unit of administration was the village. From pre-Maurya times a collector of taxes was put in charge of a group of villages. In the village itself, the lowest level of all in the pyramid of government—as it still is today—were the headman and the council. Usually the headman inherited his position but he could be replaced at the king's discretion. His 'salary' consisted of tax-free land or some benefit in kind. In large villages, the headman would be assisted by a small staff—book-keeper, watchman, and suchlike, who were paid in the same way.

The village council, though we know it was a widespread institution in early India, did not have the approval of the majority of the law books. In fact, most ignored its existence altogether. This is because the village council was not considered to be an integral part of the administrative system. Because of this we know very little about their composition or function during the period covered by this book. It is reasonable to assume that the council was made up of influential inhabitants, though there are cases where members were appointed by lot. The village council was a more developed institution in the south than it was in the Āryan heartland of the north. But, everywhere, it represented in some measure a genuine popular involvement in the running of the community.

Taxation

Most civilisations developed a system of taxation very early in their history. India certainly had a regular one before the time of the Mauryas. In an agricultural society, the principal tax is upon the land. The state took a share of the farmers' produce. What that share should be differed from law book to law book and, of course, according to the varying rapacity of kings. A sixth share was suggested in one place. The *Arthaśāstra* advised a quarter or even a third. In Maurya times, it seems to have been a quarter, even under such paragons as Aśoka. Normally, the tax was paid in the form of produce, but there were exceptions. After a bad harvest, for example, tax might be remitted altogether. There might be tax exemption as an incentive for a village to carry out an irrigation project or to extend the area of land under cultivation.

In theory, women, children, students, scholarly brāhmans, and ascetics were not to be taxed, but in practice they were not always exempt. Those sections of society which were assumed to be very low on the social scale often had to pay higher taxes than others. There were a large number of taxes, payable on practically everything from houses to potters' wheels. There were dues for using water from a canal. The *Arthaśāstra* suggested a kind of purchase-tax, ranging from a twentieth of the value for such things as sugar, oil, grain, and cloth, to a fifth on certain luxury goods. Craftsmen were supposed to pay tax in the form of one or two days' work a month, though in practice they probably paid some amount in cash.

Taxation was always—as it still is, of course—a heavy burden even under a just king and a fair administration. Under tyrants, taxes frequently became so oppressive that whole communities would leave their homes to escape the men sent to collect them. All the textbooks advised the king to take care not to overtax the people to such an extent that civil disobedience might endanger his security or threaten to stifle trade.

The justification for the king's *right* to tax his people was that the king was the virtual owner of all the land and water. Tax was therefore really a kind of rent. Not all textbooks support the doctrine of the king's ownership. Some maintained that taxation was a payment for the king's protection, and in Buddhist tales about the origin of kingship it was explicitly stated that the king was not entitled to tax his people unless he actually gave them protection.

Whatever the theory, it did not make much difference in practice. The king got his share and if he accepted (as he usually did) the best advice from the writers of textbooks, immediately put a sixth of the income into his treasury; experts all agreed that a well-filled treasury was the king's best support. The result of following this advice was to tie up in the vaults large sums of gold and silver and precious stones which offered a profitable incentive for invasion by less wealthy kings. Apart from the sixth destined for the treasury, the revenue—according to a late textbook—was to be divided between military expenditure (one-half), the king's personal needs (one-twelfth), charitable or religious work (one-twelfth), and civil service salaries (one-twelfth). How the remaining twelfth was to be disposed of is not clear, but it was probably meant for public works of one sort or another.

48

Law, Crime, and Punishment

The foundation of the law in early India was summed up by the word *dharma*. It has many meanings (to Aśoka it meant 'righteousness') and cannot be precisely translated. In a legal context only, the word is rendered here as 'Sacred Law', to emphasise its traditional importance, and its meaning—of a divinely inspired standard of correct conduct, which varied, of course, from class to class and from caste to caste. The king's primary function was to maintain and protect the Sacred Law. Naturally, he needed some guidance, not only on what exactly the Sacred Law said but also on how it should be maintained. A series of commentaries had been compiled in quite early times to elucidate the old sacred texts. One of these, the *Dharma Sūtras*, was probably composed between the sixth and second centuries BC. In the early centuries of the present era, the Sūtras, which had been written in prose, were expanded in verse. These are known as the *Dharma Śāstras* ('Instructions on the Sacred Law'). The earliest of them was that of Manu (final form second or third century AD). Together, the Sūtras and the Śāstras

19 A royal official. His skirt is folded to make a purse

codified, and commented upon, traditional ideas of great antiquity. Altogether, there seem to have been about 7000 works in the two collections, though only a small proportion of these have survived. This type of legal literature was the work of brāhmans and was composed with an overriding sense of class interest. Though other laws were accepted as necessary in an evil world—laws of contract, custom, and those made by the king—the Sacred Law took precedence. In two surviving law books (of which the *Arthaśāstra* is one) this was not accepted; the king's law was said to be the most important. But these works were exceptions written in times of strong royal authority.

All the texts insisted that the king's responsibility for maintaining the Sacred Law was overwhelming. Indeed, if the king failed in this duty he would suffer for it in the next life. In this life he was expected both to judge and to punish, for a crime unpunished was a duty unfulfilled.

In spite of the somewhat rosy view held by foreign travellers— Megasthenes, for example, said that crime was almost unknown in the empire of Chandragupta Maurya—the law books themselves offered a more realistic picture. Not unnaturally, in periods of great social change and political anarchy there is considerable crime. The history of early India was one of continual social change and frequent anarchy. Even when a strong central authority was in control, crime was rampant. The *Arthaśāstra* suggested that curfews should be imposed in towns in order to reduce burglary and violent robbery. There is plenty of evidence that the countryside was overrun by bandits. When powerful kings ruled, lawlessness was no doubt kept under control—a state of affairs which probably accounts for the glowing reports of foreign travellers. In such periods, the police administration was substantial and efficient. Local officers and military commanders were responsible for the suppression of crime and were aided by a large number of police, soldiers, and secret agents. In village and town there were official watchmen to keep guard at night. During the Gupta period, the village security and police force consisted of one elephant, a chariot for the commander, three armoured cavalrymen, and five foot-soldiers.

The criminal having been caught, justice had to be done. Though the king was the ultimate judge, and at one time in the smaller states, had actually administered justice and even punishment himself, in large countries he delegated his authority. The king remained the judge and final court of appeal only in cases of serious crimes against the state. Other courts were usually presided over by more than one judge. The *Arthaśāstra* suggested three as a suitable number. A fourth-century AD play, *The Little Clay Cart* (*Mṛcchakaṭika*), by the dramatist Śūdraka, which gave a realistic description of town life, included a court scene in which there were a chief judge, a rich merchant, and a representative of the caste of scribes on the bench. The word used for the chief judge suggests that he was a state official while the other two were unpaid magistrates.

The standards expected from judges were extremely high and they were continually watched for signs of corruption. The *Arthaśāstra* even suggested that the impartiality of the court should be tested by secret agents posing as litigants attempting to bribe the judge. It was, of course, a very difficult task to ensure the honesty of witnesses, though heavy punishments in the present life were reinforced by the threat of many unpleasant rebirths. Some classes were not normally allowed to give evidence at all, though there were a few exceptions in cases of serious crime. In civil cases women, learned brāhmans, state employees, minors, debtors, those who had committed a crime, and cripples were prohibited from giving evidence. The evidence of witnesses of low caste was not acceptable against people of a higher class.

If the judges were convinced of the guilt of the accused, but if there were insufficient real proof, they could order him to be tortured if he refused to confess. Generally speaking, the torture was not extreme. In practice its extent actually depended upon the toughness of the accused. Theoretically, brāhmans, children, the old, the sick, the insane, and women in pregnancy were not tortured, and other women only to a mild extent. In some cases, the accused could be put to 'the ordeal' though the early law books did not favour this. The ordeal could be by fire or water, as in Europe in the Middle Ages, or by touching a red-hot ploughshare with the tongue. The last was presumably based upon the assumption that a guilty man would be nervous and have a dry mouth; he would therefore burn his tongue. An innocent man, with plenty of saliva, would have a wet tongue and would therefore escape burning.

One thing at least was spared the litigants in the courts of early India— there were no lawyers.

The very ancient customs of blood-money and religious penance lay behind the system of punishment in early India. The early sūtras gave a list of fines for murder—10 cows for the murder of a śūdra or a woman of any class, 100 for a vaiśya, and 1000 for a kṣatriya. The killing of a brāhman was of such enormity that no fine could expiate it. In time, the original purpose of blood-money—to prevent physical vengeance—was forgotten, but fines as punishment played an important part in Indian justice. In general, all but the most serious crimes could be paid for in cash or in property, thus contributing to the revenue of the state. A person unable to pay the appropriate fine had to work it off. But fines were not the only form of punishment; there were certainly prisons in early India and the conditions inside them were generally very bad. Forced labour in state mines is also mentioned. Nor was mutilation unknown. Punishment of these kinds was considered to cancel out the crime entirely, so protecting the criminal from suffering the consequences of such actions in the next life.

A large number of crimes were punishable by death. The *Arthaśāstra* included murder among them. But death was also the penalty for burglary, for spreading false rumours, and for stealing the king's elephants. Even the manner of death differed for different crimes. Those mentioned above brought death by hanging. Others—such as trying to force an entry into the king's harem, murdering a close relative or ascetic, or (appropriately) arson—were punished by the criminal being burnt alive. A civilian caught stealing from the army was supposed to be shot to death with arrows. The most common form of execution, however, was impalement.

There was certainly opposition both to capital punishment and to mutilation and torture, but even the mild and humanitarian Aśoka did not abolish them. In Gupta times, however, Fa-hsien reported that most crimes were punished by fines and, though he was inclined to exaggerate, it does seem that executions were very rare. Hsüan Tsang, writing 200 years later, said that there was no capital punishment in Harṣa's empire, although he did report that criminals were left to rot in dungeons.

Naturally, brāhmans claimed amongst their many privileges that of being above the law. In practice, this probably meant that they were treated more leniently than others. The early law books laid down a scale of punishments according to the class of the offender on the principle that, as men were born unequal, there could not be equality of punishment. The *Arthaśāstra*, however, did not exempt brāhmans from capital punishment for certain crimes and there is sufficient evidence to show that brāhmans were not always above the law even if they always claimed to be so.

3 The Daily Round

VILLAGE

In early times, as in the India of today, the majority of the population lived in villages, and though surprisingly little has changed in the *appearance* of the village itself there are considerable differences in the kind of country-side which surrounds them. Today, much of the forest and jungle which covered India has disappeared, cleared for fuel and for cultivation. A typical village in the period covered by this book was surrounded by a wall or stockade designed to keep out not only marauders but also the

20 Reconstruction of an Indian village

wild animals—tigers, lions, and elephants—that roamed the countryside in large numbers. The walls of the village usually formed a rectangle pierced by four large gateways and four small ones. The large gateways were closed by a sort of portcullis, and it was through these that the cattle were driven back in from the fields at night.

Inside the walls, the village houses followed a roughly geometric pattern, though in a really small village they were grouped around a well or pond near which was a small open space shaded by trees. Houses varied in size and shape according to the class of the owner, but most were of one storey with a floor of well-beaten earth and walls of mud covered with an outer mixture of lime, earth, and cow-dung (which was believed to have purifying qualities). There would usually be only one window, very narrow and covered with a wooden lattice. The roof was of leaves, reeds, or matting made from long grasses, supported on a framework of bamboo. The inside of the house was divided into rooms by bamboo mats hung from the roof. There was a bedroom, facing north, a store-room, and a room in which to receive visitors.

21 Woman and children in front of a village hut

54

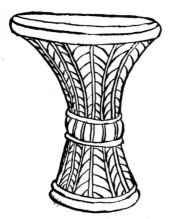

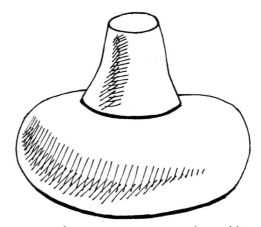

22 A rattan table in the form of an hour-glass

23 Earthenware water pot, with a goblet inverted over it

The rooms themselves were bare. In the bedroom the base of the bed, framed in wood or bamboo and set upon four legs, was a criss-cross of cords, sometimes covered with matting or a thin blanket. There were no chairs or raised seating as everyone sat on the floor. Instead of a table, a basket-work stand of thin cane shaped something like an hour-glass would hold a tray. In the store-room and kitchen, provisions—of which oil, ghee, peppers, spices, and honey were the basics—were stored in earthenware or copper pots. The larger ones could be conveniently stacked on top of one another, the base of one forming the lid of the one below; the smaller pots were usually hung in nets from the roof. These pots were only used for storage or for cooking, never for eating from. Instead, large leaves were used as plates and thrown away after a meal. If someone ate from an earthenware bowl, it had to be broken afterwards; the Law laid down that no vessel or plate could, for ritual reasons, be used twice.

The food eaten by villagers was simple and plain and very much the same as that eaten by their descendants today. A dish might consist of meat and vegetables flavoured with spices and eaten with boiled or fried rice. Flat cakes of flour—the modern *chapāti*—were eaten with spiced curry. For drinking there was water, milk, or whey. Though the richer villager would have his food fried in ghee—made by melting butter, separating the impurities and leaving the butter-oil (which did not go bad in a hot climate)—the poor had to be content with oil made from sesamum or mustard seed. The very poor were compelled to use oil of safflower, a kind of thistle.

As the village was almost a self-supporting community, variations in diet were dictated by the land itself. Wheat and barley would grow at any time in the cooler parts of the north and in the winter elsewhere. In the plains, where water could be used for irrigation, rice was a staple crop. In the drier areas such as the Deccan plateau, millet was the usual crop. Nearly everywhere there were sugar-cane, leaf vegetables, and gourds of various kinds, as well as sesamum. Pulses—peas, beans, and lentils—were common throughout India. The south, the granary of spices, sent pepper, cardamom, ginger, and cinnamon all over India.

Among fruits, the most widespread was the mango. In the wetter parts of India, the plantain, the Indian banana, flourished. In the drier regions of the west, the date-palm was cultivated. The tamarind, sour and refreshing (and also laxative in its effect), was used to flavour curry.

24 A *yakṣa* picking mangoes

25 Humped bulls

Along the coast, the palmyra and talipot palm provided material for writing upon, for making fans, and for distilling the alcoholic drinks known as toddy and arrack. The areca palm was also widely cultivated, firstly in the south and then, some time early in the present era, in the north. The nut of the areca, broken up, mixed with lime and spices, and wrapped in a leaf from the betel vine, was chewed after a meal to help digestion. It still is today. It has been suggested that chewing betel was originally a low-class habit taken over by the upper classes. Certainly the practice was widespread in Gupta times.

It is highly improbable that meat at any time formed an important part of the villager's diet. The prohibition against the killing of cows certainly did not mean that everyone was automatically a vegetarian, though, by the time of the Guptas, many upper-class people did not eat meat of any sort. The *Arthaśāstra* regarded meat-eating of all kinds as not only acceptable but commonplace, and though villagers probably came to respect the cow, they ate other meats when they were available.

There were professional hunters who supplied the rich in the towns, and villagers also went after the abundant game of forest and jungle. Like the professionals they would use bows and arrows, a javelin, or a blow-pipe with a poison dart. Or they might make traps consisting of a piece of bamboo with one end stuck in the ground and a running noose at the other. The bamboo was bent forward and baited inside the noose. When the animal took the bait the bamboo sprang upright, tightening the noose around the prey. Professional hunters used rather more elaborate devices.

Birds, too, were professionally hunted for caging as well as for eating. On the coast, villagers would not only fish for themselves but would dry their catch and supply villages and towns away from the sea.

But the majority of India's villages were inland and dependent upon working the soil. Most of the peasants, to all intents and purposes, owned their land, though the king himself was assumed to have the final proprietorial right. Most peasant holdings were small, providing barely enough to keep one family, but there were also great estates and substantial farms worked by hired labourers. These men, some of whom had lost their own land for one reason or another, were greatly despised. It was assumed that misfortune of this sort was a punishment for some sin committed in a previous existence. While some large estates grew larger, others became smaller. This was because of the customary practice of dividing up family property on the death of the head of the household. In a comparatively short period, a few generations, a large estate could be broken down into tiny plots of land.

26 An antelope caught in a hunter's trap

Whatever the size of the holding, the climate and the seasons in India, as elsewhere, imposed their own rhythm and their own needs. The most important of the latter was water. Indians appear to have learned very early the techniques of sinking deep wells, of constructing canals, and devices for controlling the flow of water from the rivers. Many of these techniques are still in use today. One of the ways of raising water was by using a leather bucket fixed to one end of a horizontal pole whose other end carried a weight. This was fixed to an upright pole at the point of balance. With this device, water

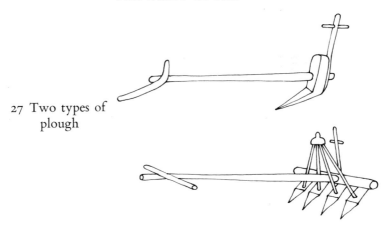

27 Two types of
   plough

could be bailed out of one irrigation ditch into another. The counter-balanced bailing bucket was operated by manpower. Another method made use of oxen. By climbing up and down a sloping ramp the animals could draw up bucketfuls of water from a well, repeating the process until their overseer called a halt.

Some irrigation works were very extensive. Kings regarded the construction of reservoirs as part of their duty to protect the people. One, at Girnar in Kāthiāwār, was originally excavated by Chandragupta Maurya, improved by Aśoka, and reconstructed by Rudradāman (see p. 16) in AD 150. The dam was rebuilt, apparently for the last time, in AD 456 by a provincial governor during the reign of the Gupta king, Skandagupta. There were undoubtedly many others, all trace of which has since vanished.

Early travellers from outside India were surprised by the fertility of India's soil and the efficiency of the peasants. The Greeks, particularly, were very impressed by the fact that the land could be made to produce two crops a year. Rice, for example, could be grown both in the rainy seasons and, with the aid of irrigation, in the dry winter. The Indian farmer knew about the uses of natural fertiliser and the *Arthaśāstra* indicated in its rules for organising the king's farms that agricultural techniques were quite highly developed. Crop rotation and the fallowing, or resting, of land was normal practice.

In early spring, the peasant would break the soil with a shallow wooden plough drawn by two oxen. The design of the plough changed very little over thousands of years, though there is mention in early literature of the use of iron ploughshares. Of all the crops grown in early India the one calling for most effort was rice. Rice needs a great deal of water—the fields must, in fact, be flooded—and seedlings have to be thinned out, a back-breaking job under the hot sun. When, at the end of autumn, the rice crop was harvested it was cut with a curved, wide-bladed sickle, then threshed by hand. After winnowing by tossing it in the air, the grains were dried in the sun, taken to the village, and poured into great jars which, after sealing, were stored in the communal granary.

Between the ploughed fields and the village itself lay the vegetable gardens and the fruit orchards. Beyond the ploughed fields was the grazing for the village cattle and the rams and sheep which supplied wool. Cattle represented both real and symbolic wealth. The number of cattle owned by a man was often an indication of his standing in the community. The cattle themselves were indispensable to the village economy as they were used for ploughing, transport, and food. Their skins could be adapted to all sorts of useful purposes. Villagers would employ a communal cattle herdsman. For identification, cattle were branded with the owner's mark, and all animals were counted and ownership registered with the village headman. Every morning the cattle herdsman would drive his charges out to the grazing area. There the herdsman normally spent the day in the shade, playing on a bamboo flute. This was partly to pass the time but also to keep the herdsman awake; while he was in charge of the cattle he was held completely responsible for them. It was his duty to protect them from thieves and wild animals and to help in this he carried a bow and arrows. In the evening, as dusk fell, the cattle were driven back through the village gate into a paddock. The milch-cows were separated from the rest and put into stalls for milking. They do not seem to have been particularly productive.

The horse was a rare animal in rural India, its ownership being almost entirely confined to the warrior class. Horses were bred in parts of Sind and the north-west, but most of the horses for kings and their armies were imported from parts of central Asia. There are reports of caravans of 500 horses or more making the long journey during the dry season.

Life in the village was hard. Natural disasters frequently hit the land, drought and floods quite impartially destroying crops. Nor was it unusual for men to be ruined because the king and his followers passed by a village and demanded, as of right, that they and their transport animals should be

28 A herdsman with his cattle

fed without payment. Taxation (see p. 47) was often so heavy that it was
cheaper to abandon cultivated fields, move elsewhere, and clear virgin
land far away from the tax collector. Generally, however, the state tried
to encourage the peasant, because agriculture was the state's primary
source of revenue. The virtue of a king could be measured by the extent
of the encouragement he gave to the rural economy. But even in the best
of times the peasant, and even the large farmer, found it difficult to avoid
some form of debt. Sometimes he was able to support it, at other times it
crushed him. On the whole, the rural community lived always under the
shadow of a wide variety of threats, both from nature and from man.

In the village itself, the evening would find the streets alive with
activity. The shops displayed their owners' simple stock. Peasants

29 A woman carrying a basket on her head

returning from the fields, women carrying loads on their heads, would be passed by porters moving at a fast, shuffling trot, bowed down under baskets suspended from a pole carried over their shoulders. Travelling story-tellers and players would be looking for a suitable stage on which to act their tales. Great bullock-wagons, solidly constructed with no thought of elegance by the village carpenter, would lumber past on their squeaking wheels with, in the shafts, a pair of humped-back bullocks, their noses pierced to take a piece of cord which was supposed to quieten them and make them more amenable to their driver's demands.

The principal shopkeepers in the village—as in the town—were the milkman, the spice seller, the oil merchant, the perfumer, and the tavern-keeper. Village shops were usually open stalls set up in front of the tradesmen's own houses. At the milkman's, the freshly prepared curds were measured with a copper vessel. Behind the oilman's shop stood the oil press. The perfumers supplied incense sticks of fragrant sandalwood, oils scented with musk and camphor, salves for the eyes—usually made from black powdered antimony which was supposed to prevent inflammation. There would also be bright stains—yellow and red—to mark women's foreheads with the beauty spot (*tilaka*) which is still popular today. The red dye was also used on the palms of the hands and the soles of the feet. The pigment came from the resin of the lac-insect and the demand was such that many peasants spent their time extracting the dye and selling it to the perfumers in villages and towns.

As well as the shopkeepers, there were large numbers of pedlars wandering from village to village or employed by some local merchant to cry his goods away from the normal shopping streets.

Every village had at least one tavern, easily recognised by a large pennant flying from a bamboo pole. There seems to have been a wide variety of alcoholic drinks, but the village tavern probably only carried a few of them. Liquor was very heavily taxed by the state, but keeping a tavern was nevertheless a profitable business. The tavern-keeper did not normally manufacture his own liquor but was supplied by distillers who made their products from the sap of the palm, from coconut, and from raw sugar.

Perhaps the most important role in the life of the village was played by the craftsmen who supplied the comparatively simple needs of the inhabitants. There was considerable variation in the social standing of craftsmen in the community. The dressers of hides occupied a particularly low position even though, in the economic life of the village, it was one of great importance. They were, in fact, outcastes, because their work brought them into contact with dead animals (hunters, butchers, and fishermen were also outcastes). Apart from providing shoes and sandals, they supplied the leather 'buckets' used to raise water from wells and irrigation ditches, as well as saddles and shields.

Other craftsmen were not considered so inferior. The carpenter, because

30 A spice seller's shop

he built the family house and took part in the ritual of construction, occupied a fairly high position in the social scale. The carpenter also made wagons, beds, and toys for the village children. The mason and stonecutter had not quite the same standing. They quarried stone or salvaged cut stone from abandoned villages. Their bricks were usually baked in a forest clearing by the men responsible for looking after the trees—which belonged to the state. The blacksmith was always busy making and repairing sickles and spades for the cultivator, knives and spears for the huntsman, and metal utensils for the home. Another busy craftsman was the village potter. His methods were very simple. The clay he used came from the shores of a local river or lake and this was mixed with water, cinders, and cow-dung. The mixture was placed on a simple solid wheel set on an axle a few inches off the floor. The potter, squatting on the ground, drove the wheel by pushing the axle with his foot while he shaped the pot with his hands. The next process was also extremely simple. The pots were put out to dry in the sun and then placed in a trench interspersed with bundles of wood which were then set alight. No glaze was applied to the pots, but they were often decorated with engraved or painted designs. Most of the potter's production was made up of containers for household provisions and for carrying water. He also made dolls and other toys for the village children.

The makers of baskets and other articles from cane were very often women. They supplied the household with brooms and boxes, and with rush matting for dividing up rooms. They also made umbrellas and fans and, from bamboo, even such substantial items as covered litters.

At times it was difficult to attract craftsmen to the village. The Gupta period, which was one of considerable social and economic disturbance, was characterised by the colonisation of new land and the absorption of conquered tribal peoples into the system of caste. There was a shortage of labour—not of cultivators, but of skilled craftsmen upon whose techniques village economy depended. The most important craftsman—as we have seen—was the carpenter, followed closely by the blacksmith and the potter. To entice these specialists to settle in the new villages they were given plots of land. There survive copper plates from widely separated parts of the Gupta dominions recording grants of such land, which suggests that the practice was widespread, at least by early in the sixth century A D.

Such incentives, however, were apparently not enough to attract craftsmen from the towns and more settled parts of the country and other inducements had to be offered. Some of them survive to this day in the more remote villages. The carpenter, for example, might receive a kind of contract fee of about two per cent of the peasant's produce, plus seedgrain for his own plot of land. In return, he would keep the peasant's plough and well-frames in good repair. The blacksmith would receive a smaller share for maintaining metal tools. The potter, who was paid a still smaller share, would supply in return ordinary small household pots. The carpenter and blacksmith received extra payment for new work, and the potter for large pots. The blacksmith might also be given free labour to work his bellows. Other village craftsmen—the barber for example—were paid in grain or with a few hours of free labour on the special plots of land assigned to them.

The daily round of the villager, whether farmer or craftsman, was one of work and sleep. Only the seasons changed the farmer's routine. While the men ploughed or sowed or harvested, the women either helped them or went about their domestic duties. There was little amusement, but life was not always dull. There were often quarrels between one village and another. Sometimes these were deadly serious—as they might be in a dispute over water, but at other times they could reach the level of high farce.

Though the life of the villager was bounded by a *physical* routine, there was a spiritual one as well. No Indian, of course, would separate one from the other, for to him the rhythm of life was not divisible into compartments. His spiritual or religious actions were intimately connected with all his other activities. Religious concepts ordered his relations with other people. A whole series of religious acts controlled his relations with the gods and with the forces of nature.

Once a month, usually in the afternoon of the day of the full moon, families of all classes would celebrate a rite in honour of their ancestors (see p. 30), when they offered food to them—bowls of rice and meat and cakes. All other rites carried out at the full moon and the new moon were basically designed to ward off hostile spirits. The actual performance of these rites differed in detail in various parts of the country.

In all societies, the changing seasons have been attended by rites and ceremonies. In India, the new year usually began at the spring equinox. In the home it was a time for renewal, symbolised by a thorough cleaning

31 A covered bullock cart

of the house and the burning of herbs. It was also a time for *public* celebra-
tion. The spring festival was probably the most popular of the many
seasonal celebrations which divided up the Indian year. It was held in
honour of Kama, the god of love. Caste restrictions were usually forgotten
at this time and everyone went out into the streets and threw red powder
at everyone else or squirted coloured water from long syringes which
were constantly refilled from great jars strategically placed at street corners.
The festival (which still takes place under the name of *Holī*) was originally
a fertility ceremony involving the spilling of blood, probably human
blood. The actual blood-letting seems to have been abandoned in very

66

early times and replaced by the symbolic red powder. The festival was a time of erotic licence—which may account for its popularity.

In the same first month of the Indian year (*Caitra*—March–April), villagers would celebrate the first ploughing of the land. A large bullock-wagon dedicated to the spring sun was drawn through the streets laden with flowers and brightly coloured cloth. This took place at dusk, and the wagon would be surrounded by torch-bearers. Special songs were sung as flowers and rice were thrown at the wagon. Drums preceded the wagon and, above the noise, there would be the sharp note of the conch, a horn made by sawing one end off the shell of a large mollusc.

In the field the farmer sprinkled consecrated water on the land. In those fields which had been left ploughed but unsown, the peasant pretended to cast seed, and the ploughshare, sprinkled with water, would be left lying on the furrows. Next day, offerings were made to the furrows and the spirits whose job it was to protect them. All this was accompanied by special rites. After they were concluded, the new ploughing began, and when this was completed the sowing was started by scattering three handfuls of grain soaked in ghee. Then came a feast, and the food which was left from it was mixed with the seed in the belief that it would help to produce a large harvest.

In some parts of the country, the girls and young women would compete to see which one could go highest on swings set up at the village meeting-place. This, too, was a magical act, for the higher the swings went the taller would grow the crop. There was also a rite to protect the fertility of cattle in which effigies of a ram and a ewe were made out of dough and covered with wool. A series of offerings and a sacrifice were made over a period of fourteen days. A specially consecrated bull was also released during the period.

The time at which the first crops began to ripen and the cows to calve (around May–June) was a period of great danger from malignant spirits who were capable of blighting the crop and damaging the young calves. A festival was therefore held in honour of the 'mother of the spirits' (*bhūtamātṛ*). As this personage was believed to be a hermaphrodite who lived in the local river or stream, men dressed up in women's clothes and women in men's. The festival lasted for fourteen days and, like most fertility ceremonies, was accompanied by considerable sexual licence.

Every agricultural process had its rites and its magic. The effect of animals and insects which damaged crops was countered with magical spells. Harvesting and the threshing of the grain had their rituals. And in May and June cattle were branded—to a ritual. In fact, there was no part of the process of growth, either of animals or of crops, which did not have its appropriate magical protection.

Should the all-important monsoon rains be delayed by any significant length of time, spells for making rain were chanted; a fast was undertaken, usually of twelve days' duration; and falling rain was imitated. When the rains seemed imminent—whether in the normal course of events or because of the magical incantations—a further series of magical acts took place. In the home, the mother's and father's beds were raised higher off the ground, and offerings of millet and fruits were made. Snakes, too, were propitiated, for in the rainy season they were often forced out of their holes and were then supposed to be particularly aggressive and dangerous. Usually, offerings were made and incantations repeated every day during the rainy season.

The rains did not put a stop to the round of festivals. The acting-out of the correct rites, the chanting of the proper incantations, the offerings and the public festivals, were essential to the normal working of life. Any interruption was expected to bring disaster. In Gupta times, there was a festival dedicated to the goddess Durgā, one of the aspects of the wife of the god Śiva. An image of the goddess was placed in a cart decorated with bells and pieces of metal burnished to shine like mirrors. As the cart passed the specially decorated houses, women and girls would cover the image with flowers, grass, and unhusked rice and sprinkle it with water. Designs of coloured rice were also made at this time on flat stretches of earth.

When the rains came to an end the parents' beds were lowered. The head of the household seated himself on the earth floor with his family, and an offering to the earth was made, implying that as the rains had given it up, so man reclaimed it. At the beginning of autumn, sacrifices for the well-being of the village herds were performed. As the time came round to cut the crop, offerings were made to the spirits of the tools that would be used to harvest it.

October–November brought a festival, usually on a grand scale in the towns, but, though necessarily on a lesser scale, still a good excuse for making merry in the village. The festival of lights (the modern *diwālī*) lasted for three days. The first day was a time for ritual purification, for bathing, and for making offerings to the god of death. The second was a time for dancing and music, drinking and visiting brothels. On the last day, the prostitutes visited every house, wishing all who lived there good luck. It was also a time for buying and selling cattle, and large fairs were held in the towns.

During the festival the tax on alcohol was lifted. Anyone who wanted to was permitted to make his own alcoholic drinks. Not unnaturally, there was considerable drunkenness which, though it began in gaiety, usually ended in fights and quarrels, injuries and, not infrequently, death.

With the coming of the cool weather, there were more rites and ceremonies, one of which was always concerned with the local river, a symbol of fertility as well as the instrument of it. As the cool season came to a close, the year and a new cycle of activity, both religious and practical, began again.

32 A *nāga* king and queen

The religion of the brāhmans was that of an aristocracy, its worship austere and its sacrifices costly. For less exalted people, as the wide range of rural festivals shows, there was an invisible world densely populated with gods and demons, with earth-spirits and genii, as real to them as the visible world which they themselves inhabited. Every village had its local god or goddess, represented by an image under a sacred tree. Some of these popular fertility deities became the subject of extensive popular devotion, especially as Buddhism, in the process of becoming a popular religion, borrowed and adapted many of the popular beliefs of the time.

The invisible world was always full of activity, some of it good but most of it malevolent. One of the most important of the popular deities was the goddess of smallpox—whom Vasco da Gama mistook for the Virgin Mary when he was taken to a temple dedicated to her in Calicut in 1498. He asked the name of the image and thought the reply was 'Maria', when in fact it was probably Mariamma (the 'Mother of Epidemics').

A snake-goddess with various names protected worshippers against snake bites. There were also many snake-spirits (*nāga*) with a human body but the tail of a snake. Nāgas could, if need be, assume complete human

33 A *yakṣa* from the East Gateway at Sānchī

form. A number of royal dynasties claimed descent from the union
between a human male and a female snake-spirit. Female nāgas, however,
were said to resume their snake-like form at night. The nāgas were
supposed to occupy a subterranean world with its own capital, Bhogavatī,
where there was a great treasure, some of which was occasionally given
to humans. Snake-spirits were greatly feared. They were believed to be
able to burn up whole towns with a flash from their eyes. But they were
also protectors of the domestic hearth, and food was set for them in case
they should leave, thus bringing disaster on the house. They were also said
to be able to bring rain, primarily because snakes were seen most often

before the rainy season started. Because of the importance of the seasonal rains in Indian agriculture, great efforts were therefore made to conciliate the nāgas. Shrines were erected near known snake lairs, and offerings of perfume and food were frequently made, especially towards the end of the dry season.

In the countryside a kind of gnome or fairy (*yakṣa*) was extensively worshipped before the beginning of the present era, but the popularity of the yakṣas declined as greater gods took their place. The yakṣas were commanded by Kubera, the god of wealth. On the whole, they were reckoned to be friendly, though the females were supposed to eat children. According to Buddhist tales, yakṣas lived in large trees, sometimes in forests, but preferably on the outskirts of towns and villages or near cemeteries. Not unnaturally, yakṣas particu-larly disliked the woodcutters whose activi-ties continually forced them to move house. Yakṣas could be consulted about the future and would speak to inquirers from their trees, but they had a habit of moralising and scolding those who came for advice. However, between the yakṣas and the humans there existed a sort of contract. In return for offerings, the yakṣas were obliged to grant what was asked of them.

In villages, the tree harbouring the local yakṣa—usually a pipal or a banyan—would be protected by a fence or even a stone wall. The earth around the tree was kept clean of debris, and garlands of flowers were hung in the branches and constantly renewed. The tree itself would be coloured with red dye and sprinkled with honey and milk. Tiny lamps were always kept alight. In return for all this, the resident yakṣa was supposed to look after the interests of the worshippers. If he did not, the villagers abandoned the tree and even threatened to cut it down. But it was not wise to go too far in threatening a yakṣa, as its presence

34 A sacred tree protected by a fence

was in some way connected with the prosperity and well-being of the village. Consequently, the relationship between the villagers and the local yakṣa was something like that between a master and an unruly servant who, if really antagonised, might set fire to the house.

Yakṣas were a survival from Vedic times and were particularly associated with the god Indra through his captain, Kubera. So, too, were the all-male *gandharvas*, heavenly musicians, one of whose occupations had been the production of soma (see p. 6). They were supposed to be particularly fond of women. Their female counterparts, the *apsarases*, were all beautiful and all over-sexed. They particularly enjoyed tempting ascetics from their vows. One of them was the mother (by the sage

Viśvāmitra, whom she seduced) of Sakuntalā, the heroine of the most famous of Kālidāsa's dramas. They also raised from the dead heroes killed on the battlefield and took them off to heaven to be their lovers. There was also a group of magicians, the *vidyādharas*, who lived in magic cities in the Himālayas. They could take human shape and frequently did so in pursuit of beautiful girls whom they carried off and married.

Among the evil spirits, the most important were the *asuras* who were at continuous war with the gods. Of more immediate danger to humans, however, were various classes of goblins. The ten-headed demon king Rāvaṇa who was defeated by the hero Rāma (see p. 8) was the most famous of a class of spirits known as *rākṣasas*. These goblins hung about lonely places at night and

35 A *gandharva* in flight

36 A *vidyādhara* carrying off a woman

attacked and sometimes ate men. Other goblins infested battlefields, cemeteries, and places where bodies were burned. There were also vampires who occupied the bodies of the dead. The ghosts of those who had died a violent death and for whom the correct sacrifices had not been made roamed about and were particularly dangerous to their surviving relatives. It seems highly probable that many of the attitudes and activities assigned to demons and goblins had their origins in those of the wild tribes which throughout the period covered by this book—and later—preyed on settled communities, stealing cattle and people for human sacrifice.

Not only gods and demi-gods were worshipped, for, according to the Indian view, the whole of nature was in some sense divine, part of an indivisible life uniting the animal, vegetable, and mineral worlds. There were sacred trees, and certain grasses and herbs were also held sacred. Hills and mountains—especially the Himālayas, home of the gods—were objects of veneration. Stones and rocks were thought of as the homes of spirits, and rivers and lakes all had some degree of sanctity. Minor

73

deities lived in them, as well as great. Every village stream and pond had a tutelary spirit. Great rivers such as the Ganges, which sprang from the foot of the god Viṣṇu, were personified; the Ganges was a goddess, as was its tributary, the Jumna. There were even sacred cities.

Animals, because they, too, were subject to the law of transmigration and were believed to have souls like men, were treated with special respect. The cow, though not yet the subject of worship, was highly regarded because 'the five products'—milk, curds, butter, urine, and dung —all had great purifying qualities and were essential to ritual.

The bull was later worshipped as the mount of the god Śiva, although the horse, which had occupied a special place from the time of the Vedic horse-sacrifice, was not the subject of a popular cult. Both the elephant and the monkey appeared in popular tales. The elephant became personified as the god, Gaṇeśa, the patron of learning, but there is no extant reference to him earlier than the fifth century AD; he was probably an extension of an earlier elephant god. The monkey god, Hanuman, who in the *Rāmāyaṇa* was the friend and servant of Rāma and was able to fly 'like an arrow through space', was again the personification of a well-established folk-figure. Other animals—the jackal and the dog, for example—were despised and feared. Birds, because at least in one sense they were of the sky, had their pleasant, oracular, and amorous functions —transmitting messages between lovers or from the gods.

All the minor demi-gods and spirits were part of the world of popular imagining. There was no separation between the mundane and the miraculous. Spirits in human form roamed the earth and were, not infrequently, encountered by men; they could be identified by various signs. Naturally, not everyone was capable of interpreting these, but there was always somebody who was, and who could advise on what should be done. There was invariably some sure counter-magic to deflect ill-luck or disease, for, though the world of the peasant may have been one of constant threat, it was also one in which there was an appropriate protection for every danger.

TOWN

From the descriptions of early Indian towns and cities it is obvious that they were no haphazard collection of buildings surrounded by fortifications but examples of careful town-planning. The *Arthaśāstra* gives very

37 An assembly of demons

precise details for the layout of cities, and such excavations as have been carried out tend to confirm that a square or rectangular grid plan was usually preferred. The siting of cities seems to have been consistently—and for obvious reasons—near the banks of a river.

The Maurya capital of Pāṭaliputra, as described by Megasthenes, occupied a narrow strip of land along the river Ganges measuring about nine miles long by only one and a half miles broad. It was surrounded by an immense wall of timber with loopholes for archers and a deep, wide moat. At intervals, there were watch-towers—over 500 of them—and there were sixty-four gates, each with its own bridge or causeway across the moat. The moat itself functioned both as a drain and as a reservoir and must have been the source of much disease. Each of the bridges was approached—as in the villages—by a portico of stone or wood consisting of two pillars and one or more crossbars.

Megasthenes' description of Pāṭaliputra is brief, but fortunately it can be expanded from other sources. Though none of these refers specifically to the Maurya capital, their descriptions are no doubt representative of architecture of the time. On the gateways at Sānchī (88), for example, there are a number of towns carved in bas-relief. On the outside of the moat of these towns, there is the characteristic railing, common also to village architecture. The main gateway is a vast building in itself standing two or three storeys high, made of wood covered with clay.

The gatehouse contained various offices, including that of the collector of tolls. There were balconies to the rooms and the windows were covered

75

with fretted screens of bamboo. The roofs were barrel-vaulted and covered either with thatch or with curved tiles. The top storey usually housed the city granary and was lit by gable windows, whose supports were decorated with paintings. The roofs themselves were ornamented with finials, either of wood or terracotta.

Passing through the gateway and into the town, the visitor or returning townsman came first to the *ratna*, a tall column of wood, stone, or metal topped by a piece of sculpture or a wheel resting on a bell-shape. These columns were a symbol of the king's authority and protection. On occasion, edicts—like those of Aśoka—were inscribed on them.

The two most important buildings in the city were the king's palace and the temple. An avenue stretching from the main eastern gate to the main western one led to the centre of the city where the palace stood, surrounded by its own fortifications, towering over the adjoining houses. Near to the palace lay the principal temple, sometimes an entire city in itself. Ideally, the main streets of the town—three going from east to west and three from north to south—crossed one another at right angles and joined a boulevard which followed the line of the city wall, thus dividing the city into sixteen sections in which the various classes making up the community were segregated. Travellers' reports and archaeological excavation have shown that, as in so many things, the ideal was by no means always achieved and that streets often meandered in anything but straight lines.

The sixteen sections were criss-crossed by other streets and lanes. The main streets were very wide, paved with cobbles, and had gutters running down the middle. But the side streets and lanes were narrow, the latter dark and dirty. The lanes were for the use of untouchables—the sweepers and removers of refuse—men too unclean to be allowed to mingle with the upper classes on the main streets. In Gupta times, if one of these people found himself forced to walk in a public street, he was compelled to keep to the extreme left.

In theory, anyway, the city was divided into eighty-one blocks. In practice, there was some segregation according to caste and function so that each community had its own temples, its own gods, and its own sacred trees. The poorer classes lived very much as they did in the villages —in single-room huts of wood, or reeds and mud, with the characteristic barrel roof thatched with straw. The rich, on the other hand, lived in considerable luxury. A typical town house was probably like a smaller

38 Reconstruction of the main gateway of a town

version of the king's palace. There would be several storeys—in fact, there are references to seven, and even eleven, which seems improbable. They would most probably have the ubiquitous barrel roof, certainly until Gupta times when a flatter type began to be popular. There were windows and balconies, whitewashed walls and painted pictures and ornamentation, sometimes in relief. The street wall was usually blank, and the space between the wooden frames of the structure might be filled with *chunam*, a kind of plaster painted a blinding white. Usually, a large house was built around a courtyard with a pool in the centre and a veranda surrounding the courtyard. The house would normally be separated from its neighbour by gardens, surrounded with walls pierced by gates very like those at the entrances to the city.

In the construction of houses—both in city and in village—there was a special ritual to be followed, and it could be very expensive, for it involved not only the carpenter, but astrologers and priests. A new house was supposed to be built only when a marriage took place, but in practice ready-built houses could be bought. If, as was most common, a house was to be specially built, great care was taken in the selection of the site. It was

39 Town houses

essential that water be readily available, as each family had to have its own private supply. If this requirement was satisfied the potential site was then carefully examined. First, the earth was scrutinised, as were the plants and grasses already growing in it. Two types of grass, *kuśa* and *darbha*, had been considered sacred since Vedic times and the presence of either of them was a sign that those who occupied the house would be blessed.

The soil was tested in various ways to determine whether it would supply a firm foundation on which the house could rest. One method used was to dig a hole, under the watchful eye of a priest who would ensure that it was dug to specific measurements; if the earth removed in the digging could be put back into the hole from which it had been removed without leaving a mound on top, the site was considered suitable. If the soil passed all the primary tests, there was still one more to go.

The priest would crumble the earth in his fingers, then taste a little on his tongue, then smell it, and finally determine its colour. Only white earth was good enough for a brāhman, but yellow was most suitable for a kṣatriya. If the earth passed all these stringent tests, a ceremony took place, during which a trench was dug and a lustration poured. This was supposed to preserve the firmness of the soil—a wise precaution, when rain might undermine the foundations of the house. After this, the priest would chant some verses designed to drive off malignant spirits, instructing them to go elsewhere as the land now belonged to the new householder. The owner then, at last, received the land from the priest and preparations could begin to make the site ready for actual construction of the house.

This, too, followed a specific course. The earth had to be turned over and watered, and the seeds of beneficent flowers had to be sown and plants bedded in. For a fixed number of days, their growth was carefully watched. Then the earth was turned again, levelled off, and brushed carefully with a broom. While all this had been going on, the carpenters had been preparing the frame of the house, each piece numbered for easy erection. Different kinds of wood were used, each with some special quality which would protect the house and its occupants. Astrologers were also at work, deciding on a day when all the omens would be suitable for construction to begin. When this was arrived at, it was the priest's turn once again. Prayers were offered at each corner of the site. Holes were dug at these corners to take the main posts. Two more holes were then dug in each side and another in the centre. A twig dipped in ghee was placed in each hole.

Actual construction began with the door-posts. These were settled first and sprinkled with water by the priest; next came the rest of the posts, starting with the south side, then the west and north. The centre pillar, which supported the roof, was the subject of an even more elaborate ritual in which the priest called upon the pillar to stand solidly in the earth. The next step was the filling-in of the walls. No window in any side of the house was supposed to be in line with one on the opposite side. The main door was never to face the west, for that direction was always associated with the dead. The door itself was fixed in and closed as soon as possible to prevent evil spirits from finding their way into the house. Throughout all stages of the remaining work, the priest said the prayers assigned to each operation. The hearth was constructed, and the family altar. Then, eventually, the roof was put on. A fence was erected around the house and the owner touched the pillars, making an incantation to each and an offering to the god of the trees at the foot of the central pillar. With final prayers for the happiness of the new occupants, a goat was sacrificed, gifts were distributed to the workers, and the new house was ready.

Inside the house, the various floors were reached by staircases of brick, stone, and sometimes marble. Occasionally, the stairs were movable and made of wood decorated with coloured stones. Windows were covered with lattice screens and heavy shutters. Cages of singing and talking birds would be placed in the openings. As in the simple village houses, rooms were separated from each other by bamboo or rattan mats, or, in wealthy households, by strips of coloured cloth. There would be carpets on the floors and statues of metal and ivory set in niches in the outer walls. Outside the main house, there were a number of other buildings—guest-rooms, store-rooms for foodstuffs and wine, the stables and, of course, the kitchen, which was always separate from the living quarters. Outside, too, were the privies, and perhaps that most luxurious of luxuries, a steam bath (see p. 132). At night, rooms were lighted by lamps made of clay with a wick dipped in ghee, or torches of resinous wood held by a servant.

Megasthenes mentioned, with a mixture of envy and surprise, that the palace of Chandragupta Maurya at Pāṭaliputra was surrounded by beautiful parks, and there are many references in Indian literature to gardens and

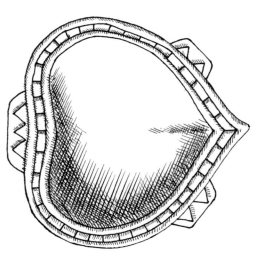

40 Top view of a lamp, showing the oil reservoir in which the wick was placed

41 A girl on a swing

42 A stylised
lotus flower

garden pavilions in which the leisured classes spent a good deal of their time. In every garden there was at least one swing hanging from a tree or from a specially constructed platform. Naturally, in a hot climate, gardens and parks required a great deal of water to sustain them and there are descriptions of ponds, fountains, and elaborate bathing pools which not only supplied water for the garden but allowed the rich to cool themselves in warm weather.

In the gardens were many flowering trees, among them the *aśoka*, bursting with scarlet flowers which were supposed to blossom only when the tree was kicked by a beautiful woman; the banana (*kadalī*), grown for its appearance as well as its fruit; the *champak*, with strongly perfumed yellow flowers; the hibiscus (*japā*); fragrant jasmines; and the most loved of all, the lotus or water-lily—not only beautiful but the subject of both religious and secular symbolism. Private gardens also had a more serious purpose than merely to delight the eye and supply flowers for garlands. Each household had its vegetable plots and beds in which medicinal plants were grown.

As well as private gardens, there were also public ones with bathing pools and fountains. Outside the city walls, there were cultivated groves of trees designed for the recreation of ordinary townsfolk. These were usually planted by kings, some of whom, like the emperor Aśoka, took great pride in them.

As the population of the towns expanded, suburbs grew up outside the walls and the lower classes were encouraged to settle there. In these suburbs were situated butchers' shops, cemeteries, and places of execution. Later, the suburbs became self-contained villages, satellite towns ringing the city. Each village became the home of certain classes of artisan, which relieved the housing problem in the city itself where it was forbidden to fill in or build on green spaces, either public or private.

The houses of the upper classes clustered around the royal palace, and in the same district were the public buildings. Apart from offices, there were hospitals both for humans and for animals, alms-houses and schools. There were also picture galleries containing murals illustrating the great epic poems. These buildings were illuminated at night and were open to all.

Close to the palace were the quarters reserved for courtesans, for professional musicians, and for the main government offices such as the treasury and the residence of the city governor.

During the day, the streets of the city were always crowded. Bullock-wagons piled high with merchandise creaked their way along, followed by caravans coming in from distant lands, officials and nobles in their chariots surrounded by men-at-arms, and groups of pilgrims, perhaps on their way to a famous temple. On the river were boats and rafts, loading and unloading goods and passengers, sometimes after a long journey, sometimes from a pleasure trip. A curtained palanquin escorted by servants might contain an old woman or some beautiful courtesan, but whichever it was, she was well concealed from the curious.

The peasant and the brāhman wore very few clothes, but there the similarity ended. The peasant with his simple loincloth and turban could never be mistaken for the brāhman with his hair shaved except for the topknot, the sacred thread over his shoulder, sandals on his feet, and a stick in his hand, with which to repel evil spirits. The brāhman also carried an umbrella. So, too, did the noble, whose long lower garment of fine cloth reached like a skirt almost to his feet and who wore another piece of cloth over his shoulders like a shawl. The cloth was sometimes of wool or of

43 A grove of trees

fine silk or muslin. Sometimes it was dyed a bright colour or patterned with gay stripes or checks.

Religious beggars, almost naked, their bodies smeared grey with ash, could be seen next to the professional beggars displaying their horrible deformities—some real and some artificial. Jugglers, acrobats, snake-charmers, singers of songs, and tellers of tales also vied for attention. Buddhist monks in saffron or reddish robes went begging, rice-bowl in hand, shaking their staffs from which iron rings dangled, keeping their eyes lowered in case they should meet the eyes of a woman even as she filled their bowl. There were many women in the streets—wives of peasants in simple skirts, with large baskets on their heads; housewives with a child on their hip. All wore a long skirt made of cloth which varied in quality according to their status and to the weather, and dressed their hair in a large bun at the nape of the neck, though, if it were festival time, it would be elaborately dressed in very complicated styles.

What women in early India wore from the waist upwards has been the subject of a good deal of scholarly argument. In sculpture women are

44 A snake-charmer and cobra

45 A woman
carrying her child on
her hip

46 A woman's head-dress,
ear-rings and necklace

almost always shown with naked breasts, though there are many references in literature to bodices and short jackets. It seems likely that these
were worn in colder parts of the country and in winter but not necessarily
in the summer. It is only in mediaeval literature that physical modesty is
demanded from women and then only from those of the higher classes.
There is no controversy over the intense delight of Indian women in
personal adornment. Jewelry was worn on the forehead and in the parting
of the hair. Ear-rings (worn, in fact, by both sexes) were often very heavy,
stretching the lobe of the ear. Necklaces and girdles were made of heavy
gold or ropes of pearls. Around the ankle circlets of bells were as popular
as they are today, but nose studs were unknown. The poorer people had
jewelry made from brass, glass, and painted pottery, and all classes wore
flowers in their hair. Both sexes used cosmetics. The most widely favoured
was a paste made from finely ground sandalwood. It was believed to be

very cooling to the skin and was sometimes coloured with dye and applied to the body in complicated patterns. Eye-shadow and reddeners for the lips were used by all classes.

City shops were, naturally, more elegant than those of the village, and their range of merchandise was sophisticated enough to attract the most fastidious town-dweller. Strictly speaking, specific quarters of the city were supposed to be allocated to various trades and crafts and the dwelling-houses of the craftsmen which lay behind their shops. This does not seem to have been slavishly adhered to, and in any case the daily markets where produce from the surrounding districts was sold usually had stands for displaying other goods. At the food-stalls there would be piles of vege-tables and fruits, prepared sweetmeats and sugar, cooked rice, chunks of meat, sauces and chutneys. In the craftsmen's quarters, jewellers and goldsmiths would be at work at their delicate trades, coppersmiths producing elegant vessels for the homes of the rich, weavers at their looms. In the street of the makers of garlands—a thriving trade, for Indians really were 'flower people'—the air would be heavy with perfume from the blossoms being threaded on strings.

The crafts of early India were highly developed. Weavers made cloth from the wool of goats and sheep, from cotton, even from certain grasses. From these materials they produced a wide range of fabrics for every purpose and climatic condition. Cloths were sometimes embroidered with gold thread, but more frequently dyed. The laundryman was sometimes the dyer as well. Though most clothes were unstitched there was still work for tailors, who made special wear for hunters and jackets and bodices for women. The highest degree of sophistication was found among the practitioners of those crafts closely allied with the arts—jewellers, gold-smiths, sculptors in wood and ivory, and the makers of musical instru-ments. Ivory was a particularly popular substance. It was not only used for sculpture but also for chair and bed legs, for dice, handles, and even for wall-covering. Craftsmen in ivory would do carvings in horn and bone, and though ivory was heavily taxed and its price controlled, there was never a shortage of buyers.

The goldsmith was expert at gilding and inlaying in precious metals. The activities of goldsmiths were very strictly supervised by the state, and a goldsmith working for a private client usually did so in the client's own house in order to lessen the chances of fraud; goldsmiths were known to be able to debase their gold with less valuable metals.

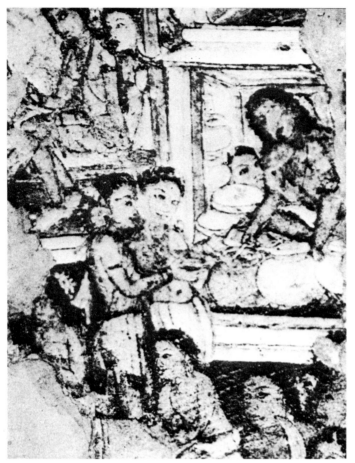

47 A seller of curds

Garland-makers occupied a special place in Indian trade. Each usually owned his own flower garden, carefully tended to produce a wide variety of blossoms and grasses throughout the year. There survive elaborate descriptions of the methods used to cultivate flower gardens, of the careful watering of the plants and the special baskets used to carry the cut blooms without damaging them. Apart from supplying flowers for the hair, they had to meet a vast demand for garlands for use at religious ceremonies and

48 A young man choosing a garland

for adorning the doorways of temples and public buildings at festival time. Flowers were used as offerings at most ceremonies and particularly at weddings. Garlands were also made from shells, leaves, fruit, and berries, and there were many well-known designs which could be asked for by name. The making of garlands was considered to be one of the 'sixty-four arts' (see pp. 99–100) and garland-makers occupied a fairly high social position.

In the cities, merchants and craftsmen were carefully supervised by agents of the state. Weights and measures and the merchants' simple scales were regularly inspected. Taxes had to be paid on stores and workshops and, in the case of craftsmen, on tools. Most craftsmen and merchants were independent workers who were assisted by members of their own family. Though there are records of large-scale undertakings owned by single 'industrialists', the most common type of enterprise larger than the individual workshop was a form of cooperative. There are many references to organisations which built temples and houses, but it is also known that cooperatives existed in other fields and operated a well-organised division of labour amongst their members. There were also corporate bodies made up of the 'industrialists', workers' cooperatives, and independent craftsmen. These were the guilds (śreṇi) which played as important part in the economy of early India as they did in mediaeval Europe.

The formation of guilds took place at a very early date and covered nearly all trades and industries by Buddhist times. The guilds fixed prices and standards of quality, as well as the wages paid to those working in cooperatives or in industrial enterprises. These regulations were considered to have the force of law and were backed by the king and the government. The state also recognised that the guild had certain judicial rights over its members. A guild court, for example, could prohibit a member from carrying on his trade. The court's power was more than economic. It acted as the guardian of its members' widows and orphans, and operated a kind of sickness benefit scheme. One indication of the guild's influence was shown by the rules of the Buddhist monastic order which stated that a married woman could not become a nun without the permission both of her husband and of his guild. At the head of the guild was a person usually called the Elder; this office was normally hereditary, but there are records of elections. In any case, the Elder was usually one of the wealthiest members of the guild.

The special importance of these corporate bodies was recognised symbolically by their possession of a special seal—a privilege usually reserved to the king and his ministers—the right to carry banners, and the ceremonial yak's-tail whisk which was an insignia of nobility. There are references to guilds possessing their own force of armed mercenaries, private armies probably used to guard caravans and trading-posts but which were sometimes loaned to the king in times of war. Guilds were often extremely wealthy and their chiefs occasionally became the

49 Scales. See also the spice seller's shop (30)

counsellors of kings. But their main function was, with the aid of a committee, to handle the affairs of a guild which might spread across much
of the country. It was the Elder's job to maintain good relations with the
heads of other guilds. Not infrequently, the Elder was a village chief as
well. As trades were always hereditary and followed by the entire family,
groups of families following the same trade would often make up whole
villages. These were usually on the outskirts of large towns and were,
in fact, overflow suburbs, duplicating the areas inside the walls reserved
to the various trades.

The wealth of some of the guilds obviously gave them a position of
influence in the state. There are indications in the *Arthaśāstra* that they
might become too powerful, their private armies a danger to the security
of the king. Guilds were sometimes encouraged to settle new lands and
there are records of guild-owned estates. Many of the guilds gave dona-
tions for the construction of temples and other religious purposes. Some
accepted deposits and lent money and were, in effect, bankers. There are
also references to investment with merchants trading inland, and even in
overseas trade.

Large profits were undoubtedly to be made in this type of business. The
commerce of India, both internal and external, was on a very considerable
scale, seldom interrupted even in periods of anarchy. Kings, as well as
individual merchants and guild-masters, profited from it. Well-established
caravan routes criss-crossed the whole of peninsular India by Maurya
times. As taxes and customs dues could be an important source of
revenue, it was in the interests of rulers to keep the roads in good condition
and to maintain ferries across the rivers. At certain periods, roads were well
maintained, surfaced with gravel, and with drains on both sides, but
generally speaking most of them were only usable in the dry season.
According to Megasthenes, roads were even marked off with milestones
and signposts. At regular intervals there were rest-houses, each with
stables for the animals, a well, and a bathing pool. Tolls were charged on
the roads to pay for their upkeep.

A journey, however, was often dangerous. Wild animals might attack
the caravan and there were many bands of professional robbers and wild
tribes. Caravans were often protected by guards who hired themselves out
to the caravan leader. This person was usually a man of some consequence
in the mercantile community, for a great deal depended on his knowledge
of roads and watering places, especially in desert terrain. Assembling a

50 Bactrian camels

caravan, particularly if it was to travel any long distance, took considerable organisation. A great number of carts and draught animals had to be got together. In addition to the merchandise, food for both men and animals had to be carried, as well as wood for the fires and water for drinking. Each night, the leader would pick a spot for the caravan to stop. If it were not near a rest-house, the caravan leader would bivouac the carts in a circle with the animals in the centre. Fires were kept lit throughout the night to fend off any wild animals, and guards were mounted. At small rivers, the caravan would cross at a ford, and at larger ones on rafts. For some reason, Indians never developed the art of bridge-building except across the moats of towns. Desert crossings were usually made at night after the sand had cooled. On this part of the journey the caravan leader would engage a local land-pilot who steered the caravan by the stars.

Rivers were also used as highways. River travel, too, was often danger-ous, for there were pirates and sandbanks and submerged rocks to contend with. But the profits of trade were high and the demand continuous. Luxury articles made up much of long-distance commerce. Spices, sandal-wood, gold and jewels from the south, fine silks and diaphanous muslins from Bengal, musk and saffron and yaks' tails from the high hills of the north. There was also a substantial trade in metals such as iron and copper, in sugar, and above all in salt from the deposits in the Punjab and the pans of the sea coasts.

On the coasts there were many ports—great and wealthy cities, espe-cially in the first centuries of the present era. There was a flourishing trade to the west, with the Persian Gulf and with Rome, and to the east with Burma, Malaya, Indonesia, and China. Much of this trade was carried by foreign ships, though there were quite a number of Indian vessels. These seem to have been much smaller than those belonging to foreigners, though there are literary references to vessels capable of carrying 700 passengers. The only reliable source, however, mentions a ship carrying 200.

Navigational aids were primitive and no different from those available to foreign sailors. Birds were often used to find land, like the dove in the story of Noah and the Ark, but steering by the stars was well advanced. Indian seamen made long and difficult journeys, taking advantage of the monsoon winds, to go as far as the east coast of Africa. Merchants established colonies throughout south-east Asia. Indian traders were well known in Alexandria, and, with Indian astrologers and prostitutes, in Rome itself. There is very little doubt that a great deal of geographical knowledge was acquired in the course of trade. In the *Purāṇas* ('Ancient Stories')— probably compiled in Gupta times but certainly making use of much earlier material—there is a considerable amount of geographical data hidden behind fantastic descriptions, by gods and goddesses, of apparently imaginary lands. The *Purāṇas* were primarily compilations of legend and religious instruction, the work of brāhmans, not sailors, but when the British explorer J. H. Speke was searching for the source of the Nile in 1860 he carried with him a map drawn according to the *Purāṇas* which turned out to record African place-names with considerable accuracy.

Indian exports to the West included ivory, both raw and carved. Precious and semi-precious stones were much in demand, and Indian merchants obtained from other countries those which could not be supplied from India's own resources. Pearls and mother-of-pearl, tortoise-shell, fine textiles, dyes, perfumes, and prepared cosmetics were all exported in large quantities. Animals and birds, too, found ready sale—the larger beasts, such as elephants, usually going overland through the trading city of Palmyra. But perhaps the most consistent and profitable trade with the West was in spices. Pepper was exported in very large quantities from the coasts of Malabār and Kerala. Most of it went to middlemen in Alexandria and from there was distributed throughout the Mediterranean area. Many of these middlemen were Arabs who had secured a monopoly in ginger, usually used medicinally in the West, camphor, cinnamon, and cardamom. Those products, such as cinnamon and camphor,

51 An Indian ship

from which an oil can be extracted were usually processed in Syria.
Indian merchants acted as middlemen themselves, especially for products
from south-east Asia and China, though there was a direct overland route
to the West from China—the Silk Road—which by-passed India. With
such a variety of goods and produce for export and re-export, there was
very little that Indian merchants wanted in return. There was, of course,
a steady import trade in luxuries; fine pottery, glass and metalware, wine,
slave-girls, and horses for kings and their armies. But the balance of trade
was strictly in India's favour. Foreign customers were, therefore, forced to
pay in gold. The drain of gold bullion and gold coins from Rome was on
such a vast scale that it was perhaps the most important source of the
financial problems of the Roman empire from Nero onwards. Roman

52 Two donors,
probably a
merchant and
his wife

gold, however, helped to construct some of the great monuments of Indian art, for many of the donors who contributed to their cost were men made rich through trading with the West.

The principal seaports were much like the larger inland towns, only with a more cosmopolitan population. There were colonies of Roman citizens in the south, and one source refers to a temple dedicated to the emperor Augustus at Muśiri (Muziris) in Keraḷa. In Tamil literature there are references to foreign soldiers in the king's bodyguard who were probably Roman citizens. Such large quantities of Roman coinage have been found at various sites in south India that it is reasonable to assume that it was probably used as a general currency in those parts.

Architecturally, the seaports would differ very little from the inland cities, though the houses of the rich may have been even more ostentatious in their design and decoration. Harbour works were extensive. At the approaches there were lighthouses, and the wharves were surrounded by large warehouses. Customs officials met each incoming vessel, examined the cargo, and stamped the king's seal on every package before it was carried to the warehouse. Behind all this commercial activity—stretching across India from the ports, along the caravan routes, to the buyers of goods and produce—there must have been appreciable financial organisation. Though there are no records of the mechanics of credit (cheques, drafts, and so on) it seems highly unlikely that all business was carried on in cash. Generally, money was lent rather than invested, and rates of interest were often enormous—10 per cent *per month* for overland caravan trading, 20 per cent for overseas. Profits must have been substantial if people were prepared to accept short-term loans at interest amounting to 120 or 240 per cent per year!

In the organisation and financing of trade, temporary associations of craftsmen and merchants were often formed. Merchant-associations probably did not trade as a body but offered various services to their members.

They did organise caravans and supply their own mercenaries to protect the individual merchants' wagons. At ports, they probably owned warehouses where members could store their goods. Local branches of an association would, no doubt, give help, if called upon, to members who were strangers in the district.

Undoubtedly, great fortunes were made in trade and there are references in Buddhist and Jaina literature to millionaires. These rich merchants formed an important element in urban society. The leaders of that society were nobles (kṣatriyas) who enjoyed certain privileges and did their best to follow the example of the king and his court in their everyday life. Rich merchants naturally tended to ape the nobles. The existence of a large leisured class, and a wealthy one at that, produced a society dedicated to the sophisticated enjoyment of pleasure and of the arts.

One of the most important sources for the life of the privileged and the wealthy is a treatise on erotics—the *Kāmasūtra*—allegedly compiled by the sage Vātsyāyana. Scholarly opinions on when the *Kāmasūtra* was written range from the second century B C to the time of the Guptas. It contains detailed instructions on erotic techniques and recipes for aphrodisiacs. Many of the former are impracticable, and the latter of doubtful efficacy. The real value of the *Kāmasūtra* lies in its evocation of the life of a man-about-town (*nāgarika*).

He would begin his day by waking in an elegant bedroom. The bed, covered with a pure white spread, had a pillow at head and foot and over it an elaborately decorated canopy. The room also contained a divan with, at one end, a table on which were arranged perfume and perfumed ointments, flowers for the hair and garlands for the neck, eye-shadow and boxes of betel. On rising the nāgarika would clean his teeth with a special root, anoint himself with perfume, shadow his eyes, redden his lips, and chew a quid of betel to sweeten his breath. Near at hand there was a cuspidor into which to spit the saliva dyed red by the betel. The rest of the furniture consisted of a chest for clothes and jewelry, a bench, a few cushions, a chess-set, a drawing-table, a few palm-leaf books, and a lute (*vīṇā*) hung on the wall. These were the basic requirements of a man of fashion. Attached to his house there was expected to be an aviary and, of course, a garden with swings and shady spots where guests could be entertained.

After his preliminary toilet, the man of fashion would bathe, either at home or in a special part of the river. Every other day he would oil his

53 An upper-class bedroom

body and have himself massaged. After the massage he did exercises to keep his muscles in good trim and then stepped into the water and washed himself with a kind of soap. After washing, he arranged his hair.

This was by no means the end of his toilet. After the bath, the nāgarika had to rub his body with perfumed ointment and paint a mark in red on his forehead and other designs on his arms. Eye-shadow had to be applied and his lips reddened again. Every four days he had to shave his face, and do the same for his whole body every fifth or tenth day. Finally, wearing freshly laundered clothes smelling of incense, adorned with jewelry, and with flowers in his hair, he was almost ready to leave the house upon the day's business. Before leaving, however, he had once more to sweeten his breath, this time with a mixture containing, among other ingredients, mango, camphor, cloves, and honey. A garland of flowers was put around his neck and a turban on his head. Then, with an umbrella to keep off the sun, the man-about-town could go off about his affairs.

If these were matters of business, they were not usually allowed to take up too much of his day. Before the midday meal, there would be time for a game of chance. This might be played with dice. The dice themselves were made either of wood or of ivory—oblong in shape, and with four scoring sides—or from the nut of the fruit *vibhīṣaka*, which has five sides. Dicing was enormously popular amongst all classes, though condemned by the brāhmans. The *Arthaśāstra* advocated the strictest government control of gambling and gambling-houses. There was also a game played on a board divided into sixty-four squares. The pieces included a king, three others—an elephant, a chariot, a horse or a ship—representing the divisions of the army, and four footmen. The game originally called for four players and the moves were decided upon by the throwing of dice. Because its military pieces and strategy suggested the movements of armies in battle the game was called *caturaṅga*—'four corps'. This game, passing through Persia to the Arabs, later spread to Europe where it became, in time, the modern game of chess.

After the midday meal, the man of fashion would, in the hot weather, take a nap. Then there might perhaps be a session of teaching new words

54 A game of dice

55–8 Four types of kiss

to his parrots and other talking birds, or watching a fight between quails, cocks, or even rams. After the evening meal, it was usual to entertain guests. There would be literary conversation, for the town-man was supposed to be a patron, admirer, and even practitioner of the arts. There would perhaps be music and plenty of alcoholic drinks. When the time came for the guests to leave, the host would present them with flowers and betel. After they had gone, the host would make love to his regular mistress and then both would walk on the terrace or the roof garden and perhaps eat sweetmeats and fruit and drink wine. Finally, his mistress would retire to her own room while he prepared himself for sleep by rubbing perfumed ointment into his skin and putting fresh flowers in his hair.

For a man of sensibility—and the nāgarika was assumed to be one—love-play was supposed to take up quite a lot of time. The *Kāmasūtra* contained advice for women as well as for men, for wives as well as concubines. Most of this advice was concerned with ensuring that both parties would enjoy the maximum pleasure. The *Kāmasūtra* suggested tenderness in love-play, but secular poetry contains many references to lovers proudly showing scratches and teeth-marks given to them by their partners. The *Kāmasūtra* is an example of the Indian passion for classification—there are, for example, sixteen types of kiss—but it treats love-play as an art and not merely as a preliminary to animal passion. In the *Kāmasūtra* young women

98

are advised to increase their attractiveness by a mixture of modesty and aggression, of tender words, fluttering eyelids, passionate embraces, and equally passionate quarrels so that reconciliation may be all the sweeter.

The *Kāmasūtra* was a textbook for the amateur. But there were, at least on the female side, plenty of professionals, too. The man of fashion had little use for a common prostitute, but the courtesan—who supplied not only sexual satisfaction but artistic and intellectual accomplishment as well —was quite another matter. Her education was wide. Apart from the techniques of her profession, she was—according to the authorities on erotics—adept at 'the sixty-four arts'. This formidable list included such obvious arts as dancing, making music, and singing, as well as the desirable qualifications of cooking, dressmaking, and embroidery. The remainder were rather more exotic—sorcery, conjuring, the inventing of riddles, fencing and archery, woodworking and architecture, logic, chemistry and mineralogy, writing in cipher, and training fighting and talking birds.

It does not seem very likely that all, if any, of the courtesans mastered every one of these arts, but many must have been women of considerable culture. Literature is full of references to them. One Ambapālī, indeed, was so famous that the Buddha is said to have preferred to dine with her rather than with the city leaders of the town of Vaiśālī which she adorned. Ambapālī is the reputed author of one of the loveliest of Pāli poems, which she is supposed to have written after she became a Buddhist nun.

59 A woman with a parrot
and cage

The courtesan, carefully trained by a professional teacher or brothel-master, was usually kept by a rich man. Her house would be beautifully decorated and elegantly furnished. There might even be an art gallery attached—a symbol of considerable financial, as well as social, standing. The courtesan lived on a lavish scale with many servants, beautiful clothes, and much jewelry. In her stables were elegant carriages and palanquins for use when she chose to go out.

Before the courtesan reached the peak of her profession, there were many people whose assistance she needed. Policemen and magistrates obviously, but also the purveyors of perfume, cloth, and garlands as well as bankers and moneylenders. Indian literature, however, continually refers to the fact that even the greatest and most accomplished of courtesans attracted criminal or near-criminal elements. They were also said to spread their favours while pretending to be faithful to one lover alone. Many of the surviving stories about them were written by moralists with a particular axe to grind. Most of the brāhman authors of law books were strongly opposed to prostitution on moral grounds, but the secular authorities were more realistic. The *Arthaśāstra* called for rigid control of all prostitutes, from the most famous courtesan to the lowest drab. Brothels were supposed to be regularly inspected and each prostitute paid a tax, amounting to two days' earnings a month, to the king's treasury. Prostitutes of all ranks were often agents of the secret police, and the *Arthaśāstra* remarked that brothels were excellent places for spies to collect information. The courtesan and the higher-class prostitute, though in theory as much subject to the law as their less prosperous colleagues, usually had powerful protectors. In the king's palace were to be found a large number of prostitutes who acted as servants, but were sometimes temporarily given to courtiers or visiting notables. They frequently accompanied the king's camp in times of war.

The early Indian attitude to prostitution was that it was a necessary element in the organisation of society. In accordance with this belief, trainers of prostitutes were encouraged by the state. Clients were able either to visit prostitutes in a brothel or invite them to their house. They were often hired as musicians and dancers for private parties. Some prostitutes lived with their mothers, who handled the business side. In the quarters set aside for them, they would display themselves, wearing heavy make-up, on balconies or at the door of the house. Business was particularly good at festival times when taboos and inhibitions were relaxed. Payment was negotiated in advance; half went to the prostitute and half to a fund used for buying clothes, perfumes, and garlands.

The man of fashion was expected also to be a man of culture. The ability to play the vīṇā was a sign of good breeding. Even kings, in Gupta times, were shown on their coins holding the instrument. Painting, too, was a

60 Courtesans

widely practised art, as was modelling in clay or wood. A talent for composing elegant verses was considered to be something of a virtue, and literary clubs held competitions presided over, on occasion, by the king himself.

Such was the world of the nobles and the rich merchants, the everyday life of a leisured class. But the city contained many other kinds of people. The orthodox lived their life according to the ancient precepts, separate from, and to a large extent untouched by the dissolute ways of the others. The day of the orthodox householder was divided between his religious obligations and his secular life. He would be up before sunrise, so that he might study the sacred texts. Then, wearing only a freshly laundered loin-cloth, he would walk into the stream in his garden at the moment of daybreak, making a prayer to the water. A few mouthfuls of water, a little thrown over his head, and it was time to adore the sun as it progressed over the horizon. After this, he oiled his topknot and recited another holy verse, rinsed out his mouth three times, rubbed his hands as if washing them, and then ritually touched various parts of his body. After another mouth-rinsing, he would meditate, meanwhile carrying out breathing exercises through his nose, closing first one nostril and then the other. After silently saying a number of incantations, the householder then stood with one foot against the ankle of the other leg. Facing the sun and intoning some sacred verses, he would make an offering of sesame seeds, flowers, barley, sandalwood, and water. After this the householder washed himself, put on fresh clothes, and applied a little perfumed oil or ointment.

At the same time the householder's wife would be occupied with her toilet, also a ritual proceeding, making herself as attractive to her husband as the family's financial standing would allow. When finished, she went to meet her husband accompanied by her children, and greeted him respectfully, kneeling down to touch his feet. Whatever the family's social standing, and however many the husband's servants, it was a wife's duty to prepare her husband's food. Before the midday meal, the husband made the first of two offerings before the domestic fire. The ritual included throwing into the flame portions of the food that was about to be eaten. He intoned prayers to the spirits of his ancestors, to the Earth and to Fire. A part of the meal was then set aside for scattering to the animals, birds, and insects. After this task had been completed the householder could eat his own meal.

There was a precise way of doing this, too. The householder took his meal alone, served by his wife. First he would rinse his hands in water. Then, using only his right hand, he would eat from the food his wife had piled up on a large banana leaf. When he had finished, he would rinse out his mouth with water without swallowing any of it. Then, and only then, would his wife have her meal served to her by the children. A similar procedure, including the sacrifice at the domestic hearth, took place at the time of the evening meal.

If there were guests at a meal, a most elaborate ritual and etiquette were laid down. The giving of hospitality was held to be one of the 'Five Great Sacrifices' (see p. 37). Whatever the original reason for this emphasis on hospitality as a religious duty, it certainly appealed to Indians, who were then (as they are today) an extremely sociable people.

The preparations for receiving a guest were complicated. A place was prepared for him to sit, and a drink was made of honey mixed with ghee or curds. This drink was also used ritually on other important occasions in the life of the family. When the guest arrived at the gate he was met by the host. A variety of welcoming gestures suitable for every rank and relationship of guest was carefully laid down. In the case of old people, such as the host's father or mother, he would kneel down and touch their feet. A bow of the head was sufficient for others, but it courteously indicated that the host felt himself to be an inferior. After the formal welcome, to which the guest responded with a blessing, he was escorted to the reception-room where a bowl of water was brought for him to wash the dust of the streets from his feet. The guest was now presented with a bowl containing the honey drink, which he accepted with both hands. He first placed the bowl by his side, then, after a pause stirred the contents of the bowl with the thumb and first finger of his right hand. After this, he drank it, following it with a mouthful of water. The meal could then be served.

Cookery in early India was certainly considered as one of the sciences. Unfortunately, no early work on the subject has survived and references in literature are the only sources available. Rice seems to have been the main element in cookery then as it is now. Long-grained rice was made into gruel and flavoured with vegetable broth; medium-grain was boiled and used in main dishes; and rice flour was made from the smallest-sized grain. Each morning, the day's supply of rice was husked, then shaken in a basket or sieve. Boiled rice would be served with curries and spices such as mace, cinnamon and cardamom, which had been carefully ground with a stone roller on a flat stone. Rice flour was formed with liquid into a flat pancake. Various pulses, beans and peas, were part of the usual diet as were a wide range of other vegetables. In some respects the food of the wealthier classes was basically the same as that of everyone else. It differed in the variety of spices, in the quality of the oil used for frying and, of course, in the quantity that would be served for a meal.

Though the Chinese traveller Fa-Hsien reported, early in the fifth century AD, that upper-class Indians did not eat meat, he probably exaggerated. The orthodox were usually vegetarian, but it seems that the majority of people were not. The *Arthaśāstra* listed regulations for the management of slaughter-houses and the kṣatriya class enjoyed not only hunting but eating what they caught. The *Kāmasūtra*, however, maintained that abstaining from meat was considered an act of merit, though it said so only as a passing comment. Among the other prohibitions contained in the sacred texts was one against eating onions and garlic. The purely social reason for this is obvious, but the prohibition does not seem to have been widely observed except among the pious.

Generally speaking, practically any kind of meat, fish, flesh, or fowl was considered eatable. Goats, tortoises, deer, parrots, peacocks, porcupines, and alligators are mentioned. There are also references to giant lizards, and their flesh was even exported to the West preserved in brine. Oxen, cows, elephants, horses, pigs, dogs, foxes, lions, frogs, and monkeys were not usually eaten.

There were various ways of cooking and dressing meat. When boiled, it was usually flavoured with sour or bitter herbs, fruit such as tamarind, or lemon juice. Meat was roasted—occasionally in the form of whole animals, but more usually as joints—on a spit, over charcoal. Sometimes meat covered with black mustard and other herbs would be cooked in an oven. It was also served with fruit. Birds were wrapped in bitter leaves, roasted, and served with a sauce of seasoned mango pulp and ghee.

In the king's palace and the homes of nobles and wealthy men, the main course of a meal was followed by a great variety of desserts. There were creamy cheeses, flavoured curds, and balls of rice or wheat coated with sugar and spices, as well as many types of fresh fruit. All the dishes were strongly seasoned, and during the meal spices were chewed to stimulate the appetite and to create thirst. To drink there were water, milk, and whey but also many varieties of fermented liquor. For the very rich, this

61 Servants husking and
winnowing rice and
grinding spices

might include imported wine; for others, toddy, rice-beer, scented liqueurs made from flowers, and a number of distilled or brewed drinks for which the *Arthaśāstra* supplied some, nowadays rather cryptic, recipes.

At the end of the meal it was usual to chew betel, which was supposed to encourage digestion as well as perfume the breath. There is also evidence that, certainly by the first century AD, smoking was fairly common, especially in north-western India where the habit may have been brought by the Kushans (see p. 15). The substance smoked was not, of course, tobacco, which was to be introduced into India only in the sixteenth century by the Portuguese. Medical works contain a number of recipes for the manufacture of cigars which were made by mixing aromatic ingredients such as herbs and scented woods with resin and pieces of quick-burning wood from the pīpal or banyan tree. This mixture, very finely ground, was coated 'to the thickness of a thumb' on to a reed some six inches long. When the mixture had dried the reed was removed. The outside of the cigar was smeared with ghee and was then ready for smoking.

A medical text of the first–second century AD warns against the dangers of too much smoking, but then goes on to advise the practice after a bath, a meal, cleaning the teeth, and so on. Smoking, however, was not recommended for pregnant women, or after drinking liquor, milk, honey, or rice and curds; this would certainly have tended to restrict a heavy smoker's diet. A later work, of around the fourth century, described the correct way to smoke. The smoker, said the author, should hold his body erect but comfortable. Three puffs of smoke should be taken at a time and expelled only through the nose.

There was always some festival or entertainment going on in the towns, many more than in the countryside where the demands of a seasonal agriculture left little time for leisure. In the town at festival times there was always a theatrical production, a dance-drama, in the courtyard or one of the side halls of the temple. These entertainments were very popular, though they were not open to all classes. One source states that 'illiterates' should not be allowed to attend a theatrical performance. Foreigners were also excluded, presumably on the grounds of their religion.

At festivals and other celebrations there were plenty of other types of amusement. Entertainers of all sorts travelled about the country performing their acts, and many journeyed great distances to attend some particularly important festival which might bring them profit. Among these travelling entertainers were musicians, bards, and singers. There were also professional wrestlers and boxers, who were sometimes hired by rich men to put on a public contest which might, on occasion, be attended by the

62 Two wrestlers

king himself. If such was the case, the ring would be set up inside the palace enclosure with rows of benches surrounding it, the whole area decorated with many coloured flags. Wrestling was highly stylised. The contestants would grasp each other around the waist and then try to break the hold or force a fall. There were many other permitted holds (62), and no doubt many unauthorised ones as well.

Teams of acrobats, complete with their own orchestra, were a great attraction. The musicians would draw the attention of the crowd and the team would suddenly build themselves into a human pyramid. Others would dance on a tightrope or balance precariously on the top of a tall pole. Javelin-dancers were much admired, whirling a number of their razor-sharp weapons in the air as they pranced to the sound of drum and flute. Sword-swallowers and men with performing animals, snake-charmers with their cobras in rattan or bamboo baskets, would also draw an excited

63 Acrobats forming a pyramid

crowd. There were comic dancers, who could produce gales of laughter just by moving an eye or making a gesture with a foot. Other entertainers displayed long pictures rolled on sticks, and told tales of great heroes or of the gods. The pictures were slowly unrolled as the story was told.

In a world in which the miraculous was believed in as implicitly as the everyday, magicians had an obvious attraction, for they could apparently draw upon the miraculous at will. To what extent their tricks were believed in would depend upon their skill and that of their assistants. There are many stories told of their accomplishments, including the well-known rope trick. In this, a tree was first made to grow from a seed. A rope would then fasten itself to one of the branches and one of the magician's assistants would climb up and hide himself among the leaves —only to reappear again, dismembered, his limbs falling one by one to the ground. The magician then reassembled them and brought the body to life by sprinkling it with a little water.

Organised games were not particularly favoured in early India except by children and young girls, who played ball-games. In very early times there had been chariot races, but these seem to have declined in popularity by the first century A.D. In Maurya times there are references to combats between gladiators. Animal fights were also very popular especially those between the larger animals such as bulls and elephants.

Early Tamil poetry contains descriptions of bullfights which seem to have had some connection, though not a very clear one, with fertility rites. The bull was not killed but wrestled with—a very dangerous affair, as the horns of the bull were left pointed. There are highly coloured descriptions of bulls dangling bloody fragments of their opponents from their horns.

Archery was a sport reserved for the warrior class, and an archery contest was sometimes the way in which princesses were married off. The hero Rāma won Sītā in such a contest. But these tests of skill were rather more frequently held for ordinary prizes and awards.

Such was life in the town. For the nobleman and the rich, it was a leisured existence with diverse physical and intellectual activities, a mannered, formal society even in its pleasures. For ordinary people there were the careful routines of work and worship, interspersed with periods of almost anarchic withdrawal of inhibitions and controls during popular festivals. Only for the pious were the routine—and the duties—fundamentally unchanging.

COURT

The descriptions we have of the palaces of kings are not particularly helpful because they usually reflect *ideal* constructions thought suitable to the *idea* of a king. Nor is archaeology of much help, at least as yet. However, it is possible to build up a picture of a typical royal palace. The palace buildings would cover a great deal of space, and they would certainly be surrounded by a moat and fortifications. At each of the gates —set, like those of the city, facing the points of the compass—there would be armed guards, while the ramparts were continually patrolled by day

64 State elephant

and by night. The main gateway, facing the royal avenue which crossed the city, was particularly impressive, decorated, perhaps, with gold and ivory panels and with sculpture. This gate opened on to the public section of the palace enclosure. Numerous buildings overlooked tiled courtyards, the passageways between them being wide enough to take wheeled vehicles. The buildings in the public section—offices, halls of audience, and suchlike—were of different sizes.

In the main gatehouse, just as in that of the city, was the royal granary. Near to the gate was a building set aside for the poor. Every day the king would distribute alms at this place; charity, especially to religious beggars, was an important royal duty. In the stables, which were also in the public part of the palace, were housed bullocks, elephants, riding-horses, and heavy, specially trained horses for pulling war chariots. Rams, too, were sometimes trained to draw light wooden or bamboo carts. To look after these animals and those in the royal menagerie, there was a large number of grooms, stable boys, professional trainers, and veterinary surgeons. All the animals had costly leather harnesses, and the horns of bullocks, elephants, and rams were gilded and decorated with colour.

Of the working animals, the horse was usually imported from countries to the north-west of India and needed considerable care, especially in the rainy season. Elephants were under royal protection; vast areas of land were made royal preserves where elephants could not be hunted except by the king, or with his permission. Capturing elephants was a difficult and sometimes dangerous job. In the first place, a herd had to be found. When this happened, tame elephants were moved into the area and a stockade was built. The tame elephants lured the wild ones into the stockade, where they were broken in before being moved to the training stables to be taught the requirements of war or how to behave in state processions.

Among the horses and elephants were one horse and one elephant which were awarded extra-special treatment. This was because it was believed that the safety of the king and, through him, of the state was bound up with their well-being. The horse and the elephant were two of the 'Seven Gems' which were supposed to be in the possession of a Universal Emperor (*cakravartin*). The idea that there could be such a personage, ruling the whole world, took hold in the Maurya period when, for the first time, one king actually ruled from coast to coast. The idea was incorporated into the Buddhist tradition and was taken over by later Hinduism. The 'Seven Gems'—signs of a Universal King—were the Golden Wheel, the Divine Guardian of the Treasury, the Horse, the Jewel Maiden, the Jewel that wrought Miracles, the General who could not be Defeated, and the White Elephant. What, apart from the horse and the elephant, all these things actually were is not known, as there is no surviving description of them and we do not in fact know if there ever was one. But the tradition of the 'Seven Gems' is still very much alive today in the Buddhist kingdoms of Laos and Thailand.

The White Elephant was not really white, but an albino with pink and yellow eyes, its skin a pale brick colour, its ears edged with white, a white tip to its trunk, and five white-tipped toenails. When an animal satisfying all or most of these characteristics was found, it had to be brought to the king. After being paraded around the city, it was consecrated by the king in a special ceremony. The state elephant was kept in a separate stable and looked after by carefully chosen keepers. The king visited the animal every day and at festival times rode on it. There are many descriptions of jewelled bridles, headpieces, and ear-rings worn by the elephant on such occasions.

65 The Seven Gems, signs of a Universal King

Rows of bells were fixed above its knees so that it would make a pleasant sound as it walked. The lower part of its legs were decorated with bangles of gold and silver.

The horse was treated very similarly and its stall was usually draped with gold and purple cloth. It, too, was visited daily by the king and when it was ridden upon state occasions its harness was covered with gold and jewels, its brow crossed by a band holding a long plume, and its saddle-cloth covered with embroidery and jewels.

Close to the stables were special buildings housing the war chariots and other wheeled vehicles. The chariots were designed to be drawn by two or four horses and were of wood covered with metal plates which in turn were covered with tiger skin. There were also chariots intended for ceremonial purposes only. These, too, were made of wood, sometimes carved, and covered with small sculptures in ivory, gold, or silver. Those parts not decorated with sculpture were painted in bright colours.

All these sections of the palace were looked after by superintendents responsible for the welfare and training of the animals and for keeping the chariots and carriages in good repair.

66 The royal horse

67 The king and his ministers in a chariot

Other parts of the palace open to the public contained gardens and pools. There were also a number of buildings, usually with flat roofs supported by pillars, sometimes made of stone but more frequently of lacquered and gilded wood. The largest of these buildings was the main audience hall. Another was set aside for theatrical and dance performances and contained sets of musical instruments. A special hall was devoted to dice and board games. In this part of the palace there were also a picture gallery and a library.

The private quarters were cut off from the rest of the palace by fences and walls. Access to them was controlled by a person known as 'the porter', who was, in effect, a very senior official. He was in charge of a large number of junior officials on whom the general organisation of the king's private life depended.

Inside the private section was kept the state treasure, which included all sorts of precious things as well as gold and jewels. Under the control of the official in charge were a large number of specialist craftsmen who valued jewels when they came into the treasury and manufactured jewelry for the king and his nobles. There were also artists and designers who worked on decorations for the palace buildings. It was also customary for

68 The royal kitchen

the jewellers and goldsmiths of the town to keep their wares in the security of the king's strongroom. Another vitally important building in the private section housed the royal arsenal, where arms were both made and stored.

The arrangement of the palace was such that the outer areas were open to the public while the central core contained the most private apartments. Between them was the hall in which the king and his council met every day, as well as the royal bath. In the same area were the kitchens and the store-rooms in which food for the entire palace population was kept. Cereals, ghee, and oil were stored in large stone jars. The kitchen itself was usually open to the air with a tiled roof set on pillars and a number of hearths arranged around the outer edge.

Descriptions of the inner apartments reserved for distinguished guests and the king's own family are so high-flown as to be practically worthless, though undoubtedly at the courts of the kings and emperors of India there was very considerable luxury. Rooms were panelled in ivory and precious metals, windows were made of crystal. From at least one of these rooms there would be a secret passage leading outside the palace and even outside the city walls. This could be used in times of danger. One source, at least, suggests that kings used such secret exits when they left the palace in disguise and wandered among the crowds in the streets listening to the gossip and complaints of ordinary people.

Near to the royal bath and to a special building in which the king ate his meals stood the king's personal quarters, with his bedroom at the centre. The furnishings were, naturally, elegant and costly. There were sofas covered with silk or woven goat-hair, and stools and chairs in bamboo and wood embellished with ivory, gold, and precious stones. The

69 Two peacocks

bed might be supported on legs which ended in reproductions of the paws of animals.

The palace gardens were, of course, the best kept in the city. In them were pools, and fishponds which supplied the royal kitchen, as well as artificial hills and islands with pavilions on them. In the gardens there were sometimes storks, chained by one leg, and multi-coloured birds adding their song to the discreet music of the palace orchestra. On hot days a water machine, which is described by the dramatist Kālidāsa, would cool the air with a fine haze of water from a device which appears to have been something like the revolving spray used today for watering lawns.

As the palace enclosure housed what was virtually a self-supporting community, it took a large number of officials and servants to run it. Inside the palace lived the principal dignitaries of the court. Foremost amongst them was the royal chaplain (*purohita*) who had probably been the king's tutor while he was still a prince and was therefore held in much respect by the king. The appointment of chaplain was usually hereditary and always went to a brāhman even when the king was a Buddhist. The chaplain, in a sense, was the keeper of the king's conscience and was supposed to advise on the morality of the royal actions. Another hereditary position was that of the general (*senāpati*) who was in charge of all military affairs. Not infrequently, he was a member of the royal family. The

treasurer, the driver of the royal chariot (who was sometimes also a bard and herald), and the page who carried the symbol of royalty before the king, were also of high rank.

Among the king's servants, his barber occupied a position of confidence even though he was of low class. Other servants looked after the king's wardrobe and prepared his bath. The head cook not only controlled the store-rooms and the palace kitchens—from which a great number of people were fed—but personally prepared the king's food. While doing this, he was constantly watched by spies and food-tasters who sampled every dish before it was set before the king and his guests.

70 Royal insignia, the fly whisk and umbrella

Other officials were responsible for the state regalia, the sword, sandals, fly whisk, the white umbrella, and the royal standard. The palace also housed a small

71 The king in his harem

army of astrologers, physicians, poets, and philosophers, musicians and
artists, who all enjoyed royal patronage because kings were expected
to be great supporters of the arts and learning. In many Sanskrit plays
there appears a character who is a kind of court jester and who is
presumably based upon a figure at real-life courts. In some, he is a dwarf
and acts as the king's cup-bearer, though the serving of wine appears

generally to have been left to women. It is possible that the cup-bearer was also the king's taster.

The most private of the king's apartments were, of course, those which housed the royal harem. These usually consisted of a number of pavilions in an area surrounded by high walls and set in beautiful gardens with many flowering trees and pools. Special apartments were reserved for the chief queen, who was the king's only legitimate wife. The chief queen's authority over the other inhabitants of the harem was usually accepted and, in the case of strong-minded queens was frequently exercised with some harshness. This was probably the chief queen's only way of protecting herself against the intrigues of the women of the harem, each of whom was always trying to win the king's undivided attention.

The harem was supervised by an official who was not usually a eunuch, as in other early civilisations, but an elderly man. He is often portrayed in literature (and in sculpture, 72). It was his duty to know everything that was going on and to make a report to the king every day. Except for this official and the king, everyone in the harem area was female. Even the guards were women armed with bows, pikes, and metal helmets. It seems probable that these guards were foreigners, as the word used for them (*yavana*) meant a Greek or a Westerner. Presumably they were slaves imported for the purpose. There were also a large number of servants, and wet-nurses for the children who remained in the harem until old enough to be put into the hands of a private tutor.

Naturally, as no princess of the harem had any other function than to be ready in case the king should select her for his bed, her toilet was of great importance. Each one had a serving-woman who would be waiting for the moment when her mistress woke up. Fresh quids of betel were prepared and placed in ivory boxes, and scented ointments were made ready. Freshly laundered clothing perfumed with incense, razors, tweezers, ear-picks, sticks of wood for cleaning the teeth, ivory combs, instruments for applying cosmetics and for drawing coloured designs on the skin, were all assembled. Boxes of jewelry and garlands of flowers were set out on trays. Musicians and dancers—all women, of course—prepared themselves to accompany the ritual of the toilet.

On waking, each princess was offered a quid of betel by the servant whose job it was to prepare it. Then it was time for her to be massaged with ointments and perfumed oils. Her servants kneaded her flesh to the accompaniment of suitable music from the orchestra. Then her hair was

72 The guardian of the harem

dressed with oil to give it gloss. After the massage, the next stage was a bath, indoors in winter and in the rainy season, but in a pool or under an artificial waterfall in fine weather. The 'soap' used was made by cutting up the fruit of the soap-berry and leaving it in water for about half an hour. After washing, the princess would clean her teeth, rinse out her mouth with a decoction of herbs in milk, and leave her bath. Her hair would be dried and a black powder was then combed into it.

It was now time for her servants to rub her body with an ointment made from ground sandalwood and to colour the soles of her feet with lac. Designs were drawn in colour on her body, her eyelids were tinted with paste applied with a little gold or silver stick, and her lips were reddened. The hair-parting was also coloured. There were many different styles for hair and ways of adorning it with jewelry, flowers, feathers, and pins. After the hair had been arranged, a beauty spot in a dark colour was carefully applied on the forehead. At this stage, the princess was ready to be dressed.

Normally, she would only wear a light skirt and no upper garment. The choosing of jewelry, bracelets, neck-chains, anklets, rings, girdles, and ear-pendants took a considerable time. The anklets were usually hollow and filled with small stones which made a pleasant tinkling sound as the wearer walked. Ear-pendants were often extremely elaborate and heavy and were held to the ear by a thick rod.

After all this had been completed, it was time for the midday meal and a period of waiting for the king. The time was filled with teaching talking birds or, if the weather was hot, sleeping. There would, perhaps, be a stroll in the gardens with other ladies of the harem followed by a bathe— which washed the designs from their bodies until the water was dyed with colour. The king might join them and each of the women would try and show him how beautiful she was by playing games which showed off her athletic young body.

73 Hair
curlers

74 Decorated
ivory combs

75 A princess at her toilet

76 A concubine paddling
in a waterfall

After the evening meal was over, all the women would assemble in a special hall, there to be entertained with music and dancing until the king joined them and chose one or more of them to accompany him. The others then retired for the night to recoup their strength for the next day —which would be just the same, a mixture of long preparation and tedium enlivened by the hope that the king's eye might fall upon one instead of another.

The king's day—if he were conscientious, or at least tried to emulate the ideal set up for him by the writers of textbooks—was a full one. The *Arthaśāstra*, which catalogued everything with clinical precision, carefully divided up the day. The king was to rise early—to the sound of the royal orchestra. After a simple toilet, he would meet his ministers and discuss affairs of state. Then he would be greeted by the principal dignitaries and officials, including his physician, his cook, the head gardener, the royal astrologer, and, of course, the keeper of the harem who would then make his daily report. After this, there was a public audience in the hall set aside for this purpose in the public sector of the palace enclosure. Complaints were listened to and decisions made.

When this *public* duty was over, the king relaxed in the private quarters and bathed, either in a pool or in his private bathroom. After his bath and after the necessary devotions had been paid to the gods, he went to his private apartment, was massaged with perfumed ointment, and dressed. After this, he would sometimes play a game of dice and then take his midday meal. This he ate alone in a special pavilion. The dishes were set on a low table and were tasted in the king's presence in case some enemy had poisoned them. While he ate, the royal orchestra played and servants fanned him. In theory at least, the king was vegetarian; in practice, he probably pleased himself. There was wine to drink and an elegant golden bowl to drink it from.

The meal would be followed by a short siesta. Afterwards, the king heard details from the officers of the treasury and reports from his secret agents. Ministers would attend to offer advice and receive instructions. With these duties disposed of, the king could amuse himself, and listen, perhaps, to the recitation of poems about the exploits of his ancestors or about the gods and heroes. He might practise with bow and arrow, play a board-game, or stroll in the gardens. Later he would visit the royal stables or watch his soldiers at drill.

At sunset, the king celebrated the evening rite and perhaps, once again, received reports from his spies. Next came a bathe, usually with his wives, then dinner with a few of them or with guests. After this, the king would sit on a terrace surrounded by wives and concubines. When it was time to retire, he left for his private apartment to sleep alone for a few hours.

The king would sometimes visit another of his palaces, accompanied by a large retinue of servants and some of the women of his harem. He might, on occasion, spend part of the hot season in a 'camp', where his routine was supposed to be the same as it was in more settled quarters. Sometimes he went hunting on horseback and with only a few retainers, although only if his ministers gave their consent. Such was the king's life —if he chose. Many kings were exemplary rulers; others spent most of their time in the harem. For the latter, there was ever-present danger of a palace revolution, and surviving literature is full of reminders of what happened to kings who neglected their duty to the state. The *Mahābhārata*, for example, explicitly advised and approved of revolt against such a king, and said that he should be killed like a mad dog. Some kings were devoted to their duties. Chandragupta Maurya had his massage while he listened to complaints in the public audience hall, in order not to waste valuable time. Aśoka insisted that affairs of state took precedence, even when he had retired into the harem.

The magical and semi-divine position of the king has already been mentioned briefly (see p. 43). It was established at the time of his consecration by a series of sacrifices and ceremonies. For these, a special pavilion—consisting of a platform with an altar, and four pillars supporting a roof—was erected. In one corner of the pavilion, the royal treasure was piled up, and near it a fire was lit. In another corner were garlands of flowers, food-grains, milk, ghee, and clothing, all of which had been given by the people. In the pavilion was set up a throne made of wood; near it was a wooden vase containing water from the sacred rivers mixed with honey and ghee. There was also a tiger skin, a wooden sword, a bow with three arrows, the horn of an antelope, some dice and the branch of a fig tree. The clothes the king was to put on after the consecration were also placed by the throne, as were a number of bowls containing the main offerings which had to be made during the ceremony. The outer edges of the pavilion were lined with vases containing blue lotus flowers. The king's chariot was also near at hand, and so was the state elephant. Near by was a white bull with gilded horns, its harness decorated with garlands of flowers. With armed men occupying the palace courtyard, with musicians and dancers assembled, with learnèd brāhmans from all over the kingdom in attendance, and officers of state and of the army waiting, it was time for the new king to appear.

The day on which the consecration took place had been arrived at by astrologers over a year before, so that a number of preliminary ceremonies could be carried out. The royal chaplain had made offerings to the deities of the seasons, and twelve days before the consecration he had paid a ritual visit to the great dignitaries of the state, to the most important palace officials, to the chief queen, and to one other woman symbolising the whole harem. The reason for these visits is obscure, but no doubt it was intended to represent the identification of the organisation of the state —and of the new king's private life—with the ceremony.

On the day before the consecration, the gates of the city and of the palace had been decorated. Banners and pennants had been hoisted on public buildings, houses, temples, and trees. Lengths of fine cloth were hung from the balconies of houses lining the processional routes. Some of the cloth was decorated with pearls and precious stones or finely embroidered. The roads the new king would pass along were carefully swept, and piles of incense and fragrant woods were placed at suitable intervals along the route. They were to be lit so that the burning wood perfumed the air as the king passed.

77 A king dining

On the evening before the ceremony, the royal chaplain paid the king a visit and warned him to fast and to stay away from his women during the night. The new king bathed and went to the temple, where he made an offering to the sacred fire and spent some time lying on a bed of consecrated grasses before returning to his private quarters.

Early next morning, last-minute preparations began. Crowds were already filling the streets and the area around the palace enclosure. In his private apartments, the new king carried out his usual morning ritual and then waited for a specially prepared chariot to carry him to the pavilion. When this arrived, he entered it and, with an official on each side, one holding an umbrella and the other a fly whisk, set off accompanied by his women. The procession left the palace and also the city by the east gate and then turned around and ceremonially re-entered the city where it was greeted by various dignitaries and the cheers of the populace. With an orchestra in front blowing on conches and striking cymbals, the procession made its way to the palace, the king's chariot surrounded by priests and ministers, by men carrying banners and other insignia, and by young girls with baskets of flowers and wheatcakes. As the procession moved along the route, the piles of incense and perfumed wood were lit, while the people on the balconies threw down flower petals, pieces of gold, and toasted grain.

The procession entered the palace enclosure by the main gate and made for the pavilion. Once inside, the king's fine clothes and jewelry were taken from him and he was dressed in a plain white robe. Offerings were made by the chief priest and the consecrated water was divided among four vases and then poured over the king. He was presented with a bow and arrows, which symbolised victory as well as the king's relationship with the divine archer, the god Śiva. The king faced the 'four corners of the world', and stated his claim to them as the Universal Emperor. At certain times during the period covered by this book, the king also took three steps on the tiger skin to identify himself with the god Viṣṇu who, in three paces, was able to cover the extent of both heaven and earth. The officiating priest addressed the gods, calling upon them to protect the king, who was—if not a god himself—at least very close to being one.

Either at some stage in the foregoing ceremonies or just after their completion, the king sat on the throne, which faced to the east. Priests, brāhmans, dignitaries of the state, and representatives of the people filed past and sprinkled the king with holy water. The officiating priest spread these lustrations over the king with the black antelope's horn, and the ceremony of consecration was over. The king was now formally presented as the king to those who attended the ceremony.

At various periods, other ceremonies were introduced and some of those outlined above were abandoned, but, generally speaking, the consecration ceremony followed a well-established tradition. At the conclusion, offerings of lotus flowers, rice, wheatcakes, ghee, toasted grain, and milk were made.

The king, once again dressed in sumptuous clothing, covered with jewelry, and accompanied by the regalia, then walked to the permanent throne which stood in the audience hall and sat on it for the first time. After this, he left the palace, riding upon the state elephant. The procession moved up the royal avenue and then made a circuit of the city, going from the east in a westerly direction. Having thus symbolically taken possession of his capital, the king returned to the palace, where he used the royal seal for the first time and issued an amnesty for all prisoners, including those sentenced to death. He also ordered liberation for caged birds. Work animals were to be rested, and cows left unmilked for the whole of the day of consecration. For the next fourteen days other ceremonies and entertainments took place, and for a whole year the king was supposed neither to cut his hair nor to shave, so preserving the hair that had been consecrated with the water from the holy rivers.

Throughout his reign, the king renewed the magical power given to him at the consecration ceremony by means of a number of special sacrifices. One of these was the 'drink of strength' (*vājapeya*), which was supposed to revive his physical vitality as well as his magical power. Another was the horse sacrifice of Vedic origin (see p. 8), which was revived at various times and particularly by the Gupta emperors.

Naturally, the king took part in a number of lesser ceremonies throughout the year. He also went on pilgrimages to important shrines and holy places. He travelled in great splendour and to the sound of loud music from the royal orchestra, and was accompanied by many officials and servants as well as selected women from the harem. During his travels, the local inhabitants were forced to supply food and sometimes labour to the royal caravan.

Another extremely important event in palace life—and in that of the state—was the birth of an heir. The event was usually announced by drummers, and this was the signal for everyone to stop work and begin to enjoy themselves. The people would send gifts to the palace, and ambassadors from neighbouring states would arrive with costly presents and the congratulations of their masters. Entertainments were put on in public places and in the palace, and there was usually an amnesty for prisoners.

The education of an heir was of great importance. His whole life was carefully supervised. His studies in statecraft were intense and included, as soon as possible, some military training. He was made acquainted with the real or imaginary exploits of his ancestors by bards who recited epic poems. When he was assumed to have mastered all the necessary accomplishments, the prince was sent off to take part in a military campaign. On his return, he was sometimes appointed governor of a province. Before this, he would have been married with suitable and extravagant ceremony, and would have set up his own harem.

In some kingdoms, the heir was officially associated with the king himself in affairs of state, and his name was inscribed on one side of the coinage. But he was automatically assumed to be a possible danger to the king and was carefully watched by spies. There are frequent mentions in early literature of the crime of royal parricide. An ageing king might decide to escape this, possibly by abdicating—a practice approved by tradition. Chandragupta Maurya is supposed to have given up the throne to become a Jaina monk and to have starved himself to death.

In early India, though the king lived in great luxury, he was always threatened by various interests which—if he gave any sign of weakness or lack of grip on affairs, either through indolence, disease, or merely old age—might overthrow him. The fear of assassination was always present. The king controlled secret agents whose identity was unknown even to his family and his ministers—who were themselves continually watched for any indications of a conspiracy. Some kings never spent two consecutive nights in the same bed. Others employed foreign guards who, it was thought, were more difficult to suborn. Even the ordinary people of the city might threaten the king if he did not protect their welfare. Behind the elegant façade of luxury there always lay intrigue, and there were always gaps in the magical defences of kingship.

MONASTERY AND HERMITAGE

According to the Sacred Law, when a householder's hair turned white and there were grandchildren in his house, he should become a hermit. It was a rather drastic way of ensuring salvation, for the life of a hermit was one of great hardship and physical suffering. The special place given to asceticism in the Sacred Law represented, in fact, a successful attempt by orthodox brāhmans to absorb into the social structure a widespread practice which had perhaps originated in pre-Āryan times. There were probably many more ascetics who had not gone through the formal stages of life than those who had. Sometimes hermits lived alone in the heart of a forest, inflicting all manner of tortures on themselves in order to mortify the body and thus release the spirit. Others lived on the outskirts of towns and villages, sitting surrounded by great fires under the hottest of suns, lying on beds of spikes, hanging for long periods upside down, or holding an arm up over their heads until the muscles atrophied.

Others lived in groups of huts under the leadership of a teacher (*guru*). Some wandered around the countryside with their begging-bowls, declaiming their beliefs to those who would listen. All were much respected, for it was believed that ascetics had acquired magical powers. The ascetic who had reached the highest levels could see the past, present, and future, and frequently visited the gods, who were also known to come down to

78 A hermit outside his
hut

earth especially to converse with an ascetic in his hermitage. It was thought
that the ascetic could destroy cities as well as protect them from famine,
disease, and attack. Above all, he was completely free of the world of flesh
and appearance. His knowledge of the cosmic mysteries was so profound
that it could not be expressed in words, though many sects tried to do so;
from their attempts grew a large body of mystical doctrine which
profoundly affected Indian religion.

The life of the hermit was, therefore, one of terrible austerity; his reward, bliss. Some ascetics were undoubtedly fakes, but most were not. A hermit could always be recognised by his matted hair, his taut skin with the bones showing through. If he wore any clothing at all, it would be a tattered rag. If he was on a pilgrimage, he carried a begging-bowl slung over his shoulder, with a water-pot and a few other objects. In the rainy season, the ascetic retired into the forest or perhaps into a cave on a mountainside.

It has been suggested that the establishment of monasteries by the Buddhists was designed to achieve a degree of institutional asceticism, one which would benefit both the individual and the Buddhist order by combining evangelism with the quest for personal salvation. Whatever the explanation, the setting up of monasteries was a natural consequence of the formation of an order of monks. Certainly, by the time of the emperor Aśoka, India was covered with *vihāras*—which were both temples and monasteries.

Some of these monasteries were, under the patronage of kings, great centres of learning. One such was that at Nālandā in Bihār, which was

79 Life in a hermitage; in the background, a small *stūpa*

80 Reconstruction of the stūpas and monasteries at Sānchī

founded in Gupta times, though it may well have been the site of a
monastic foundation long before that. Other monasteries were small and
occupied only during the rainy season. At other times of the year the
monks were usually away on pilgrimages to the holy places of Buddhism.

Early monasteries were probably groups of huts set around an open
space. From this simple arrangement developed a conventional style
consisting of a series of cells on three sides of a courtyard with an inside
veranda. The cells were constructed mainly of wood, sometimes two
storeys high with barrel roofs and horseshoe-shaped gable-ends (80). The
entrance would be decorated with fretted woodwork and a portico
supporting a balcony, from which processions could be watched.

Between the third century BC and second century AD, and during a
revival about 300 years later, monasteries as well as temples were cut out
of rock at various sites in western India. In a sense, this was a return to the
old convention by which hermits often retired into natural caves. The
difference was between nature and art, in the technical and aesthetic
achievement. A typical rock-cut monastery of the early period consisted
of a large central hall entered by a doorway in front of which was a
veranda or portico in the open air. Off the hall opened square cells for
monks.

The architecture of the cave monasteries took the form of copies—as far as it was possible in stone—of free-standing, open-air structures in wood, with all the joints and fastenings used in carpentry simulated in the stone (*81*). Wood was also used as decoration both inside and outside the cave.

In eastern India from about the fifth century AD, monasteries were built in brick. This was the Buddha's own country and there were many shrines associated with episodes in his life, such as that in the Deer Park at Sārnāth where he received Enlightenment, and at Kuśinagara where he died and entered nirvāna. These shrines with their many buildings often covered vast areas. The monasteries usually stood on a high plinth of solid brick, moulded and decorated with stucco figures.

Some of these Buddhist communities contained hundreds, sometimes thousands, of people—monks and novices, servants and slaves, as well as pilgrims. The monastery building usually followed the old pattern, being arranged around a square with a cloister-like veranda off which the individual cells opened. In the courtyard stood either a *stūpa*—a mound under which was buried a relic of the Buddha or of some holy man—or a temple.

Inside each cell was a simple bed like that used by a villager, a stool, a backboard, a spittoon, some pieces of matting, and a few cotton pillows. Everything, including utensils and bowls, was supposed to be absolutely plain and undecorated. Near at hand were a number of chapels each containing an image of the Buddha.

A meeting hall, sometimes very large and lit by lamps set in niches, was used once a month for community prayers. In this hall all the collective ceremonies of the monastery took place—from ordination of new monks to expulsion of those who had failed to keep the law. Near by, or sometimes actually in the same building, were granaries and store-rooms; and the kitchen was outside near a well. A large artificial pool for bathing, and latrines with a system of main drainage, completed the essential equipment of the monastery. In the larger and more luxurious monasteries there was also a bath-house which either contained, or had next to it, a steam-bath. As a separate building, the steam-bath consisted of a basement, a ground floor, and one more storey. The rooms were lined with animal skins covered with plaster. The ante-room contained water in large pots, the next room had a great fire burning in the centre and stone benches fixed to the walls. The bather sweated in the hot-room, frequently doused with

81 Carpentry simulated in stone. Chaitya Hall

warm water, and then jumped into a pool containing cool water in a further room.

The exteriors of all the buildings of the monastery were often painted white and richly decorated. Inside there would be sculptured bas-reliefs, or murals in coloured and gilded plaster. A great deal of wood was used for pillars, doors, and balconies. The cave monasteries, too, were decorated with painted and sculptured murals, some of which still survive as in the famous caves of Ajantā. These show a splendour which confirms both the importance and the wealth of such Buddhist centres. Many of the murals which depicted episodes from the Buddhist stories were used by monks to explain their teachings to pilgrims.

The rainy season, extending from about June to October, saw the monasteries full of monks studying the scriptures and meditating. Some of them carried out administrative duties, others looked after the gardens and the store-rooms, some were tailors and dyers or were responsible for the distribution of food. In theory, there was no superior in a Buddhist monastery. A novice would attach himself to a particular monk who would help to guide his studies and devotions and whom he treated with great respect. But the monastery was a collection of individuals who acknowledged obedience to no one except the Buddha and the way of life which he had laid down. There was no central authority which controlled the monasteries and, because of this, there was no uniformity in the way in which they were run. In practice, however, it was necessary that there be some person with special responsibility in each monastery. A chief monk or abbot was therefore elected by all the monks. The running of the monastery was left to a committee of the older monks, and it was the committee and not the abbot who decided upon admissions and expulsions. Matters of great importance to the monastery as a whole were decided at a general meeting of all the monks, and for these meetings there was a regular system of procedure laid down.

Few restrictions were placed on membership of the Buddhist order. There was no discrimination by caste, though slaves, debtors, soldiers, and others who were in some way bound to a superior had to have the permission of that superior before they could enter the order. Novices were accepted at the age of eight, but the minimum age of qualification for final membership was twenty. The rites of admission were very simple. The supplicant put on three orange or yellow robes, ceremonially had his head shaved, and pronounced the Three Jewels—'I go for refuge to the

Buddha; I go for refuge to the Doctrine; I go for refuge to the Order'—and the Ten Precepts. These were to refrain from (1) hurting living things; (2) taking what was not given; (3) evil behaviour brought on by passion; (4) false speech; (5) alcohol; (6) eating after midday; (7) dancing, singing, music, and dramatic performance; (8) the use of garlands, perfumes, ointments, and jewelry; (9) the use of a high-based bed; and (10) accepting gold and silver.

The Ten Precepts were not vows but rather ambitions, and any monk who honestly found he could not keep them was able to leave the order without criticism, though the ordinary Buddhist layman was inclined to despise a monk who could not keep the Ten Precepts. Sometimes the precepts

82 The Three Jewels, symbolising the Buddha, the Doctrine and the monastic order

were accepted for only a fixed period—even quite a short one. A few months spent in a Buddhist monastery was considered a good preparation for ordinary life. This practice is still common today in countries like Burma.

The first of the precepts did not, at least at the beginning, mean that the monks were vegetarian. A monk could eat meat if the animal had not been specially killed for him. The third precept was really a vow of celibacy. The sixth was no real hardship and in cold climates it was permissible to take an evening meal, though it was then claimed to be a medicine. The prohibition against music and dancing did not include such performances when they had a religious purpose. The tenth precept, which was in fact a ban on material possessions, was not as drastic as it might appear. According to the letter of the law, a monk was to own only three robes, a waist-cloth, an alms-bowl, a razor, a needle, and a piece of cloth through which to strain drinking water, in case he should inadvertently destroy any of the miscroscopic living things that are usually present in it. However, it was not unusual for a monk to possess much more than this, though it was excused by pretending that his property actually belonged to the monastery and that he merely had the use of it. Every morning, the monks were supposed to beg for their food and bring what they had received to the monastery. This practice, however, was abandoned in the wealthier monasteries or only carried out symbolically.

The daily life of the monks was usually spent in study, meditation, and religious observances. But they were also supposed to clean their own cells and other parts of the monastery. The older monks taught the novices. Among the spiritual exercises laid down was one in which the monk sat cross-legged and filled his mind with the four fundamental virtues—love, pity, joy, and serenity. In another, the monk contemplated all that was vile in the material world. For the adept, there were more advanced meditations.

If a strange monk arrived at the monastery he was met by a delegation of residents who would carry the visitor's possessions. The visitor would be taken to a special part of the monastery, where water was brought for his feet and oil to massage them. If his arrival occurred after the midday meal, he would be given a sweetened drink. After resting, the visitor would be asked how long he had been in the order and then allotted a cell, the position of which depended on his seniority. After this, he would take part in the general life of the monastery.

In early times, there were also Buddhist nuns. Very strict regulations existed, designed to avoid any suggestion of immorality, but this did not prevent such accusations being made by religious opponents. The nuns wore the same robes as men, had their hair shaved, and followed a similar discipline to that of the monks.

With the onset of the dry season, the monks prepared to leave the monastery, either to go on a pilgrimage to one of the holy places, or to preach the doctrine. A special festival at which laymen presented gifts to the monastery and took part in religious processions ended the period of retreat and meditation, and the monks dispersed throughout the countryside, travelling sometimes immense distances, in order to spread the teachings of the Buddha.

The larger monasteries which were also centres of learning usually had a large permanent community, which was, in effect, the teaching staff. The great Buddhist 'university' at Nālandā was visited by a number of Chinese travellers, including Hsüan Tsang in the first half of the seventh century A D. His description of Nālandā tells us that the monastery consisted of hundreds of buildings, some with great towers apparently used for astronomical observation and so high that they touched the clouds. The outside of these towers were decorated with images. There were a great many pools and streams full of blue lotus flowers. Shade came from groves of mango trees and there were flowers and flowering shrubs everywhere. Though the Chinese travellers probably exaggerated, one referred to a

83 The Buddha begging for his food

tower over 200 feet high and another to a copper image measuring 80 feet and standing in an immense six-storey building. Their descriptions conjure up a picture of Nālandā in the time of its greatest wealth and prestige. They tell of glittering metal roofs, and tiles glazed in brilliant colours, the pillars of pavilions richly carved, the beams painted red or inlaid with semi-precious stones, holding up ceilings glowing with all the colours of the rainbow. All this luxury was made possible by the revenues from more than a hundred villages. Students received food and clothing free. The land owned by the monastery was worked by a staff of labourers and, on occasion, by students.

According to Hsüan Tsang, entry into Nālandā was by a very difficult oral examination and failures were as high as eighty per cent. Teaching was carried out from a hundred pulpits, and students took part in discussions

137

with their teacher and amongst themselves. As well as study there was exercise—which consisted of walking along certain quiet and shady paths.

The students' routine was controlled by a special official who also allotted to them various types of manual work around the monastery, but all matters of discipline were left to the students themselves. The day began at dawn and the passing hours were signalled by beats on a drum. Time was told with the aid of a water-clock. This was a metal basin filled with water in which floated a copper cup. A small hole in the bottom of the cup allowed the water to enter. Every forty-five minutes the cup filled and struck the bottom of the bowl. Time was measured from sunrise, and the first division, i.e. at 6.45 a.m., was announced to the monastery by a single beat on a drum. At 7.30 there were two drum taps, at 8.15, three. At 9 a.m. there were four as well as a single blast on a conch shell followed by a drum-roll. The division then began again, except that at midday there were four beats on the drum, followed by a blast on the conch shell and two more drum-beats. The day ended at 6 p.m., the hour of sunset, but the divisions were still announced in the same way during the night.

Study was supposed to last for eight hours with lessons and discussions. On occasion, a scholar of renown might call a discussion and himself judge the standard of those taking part. If one of the participants particularly shone he would be placed on an elephant and ceremonially escorted to the main gate of the monastery. But if anybody taking part failed to satisfy the listeners that his logic was sound, or offended them by using inappropriate language, he was quite liable to find himself daubed with mud and thrown into a ditch. The reputation of Nālandā was so high that it was profitable to pretend to have studied there. It seems that it proved necessary for documents carrying clay seals to be issued to those who had actually studied at Nālandā, because so many false claims were being made.

The Buddhists were not the only ones to favour the monastic life. The Jains, whose founder Mahāvīra was a contemporary of the Buddha, believed (and still believe) that full salvation was not possible for the layman and could only be achieved after a long course of fasting, penances, study, and meditation. The monastic life of a Jaina monk was strict and harsh. At the initiation ceremony, the hair was not shaved but pulled out by the roots. Meals, the food for which was begged from the pious, were frugal and fasts were frequent.

The life of a Jaina monk was bounded by five vows—to refrain from

138

killing, stealing, lying, sexual activity, and possessing material things. These vows were kept in the strictest manner. The eating of meat was totally forbidden. No life at all could be taken, even that of insects. Jaina monks carried with them a feather duster with which to carefully brush insects from their path in case they should inadvertently tread on one. They also wore veils across their mouths to prevent them from inhaling living things. Like the Buddhists, they strained their drinking water, but in other ways they went much further. No Jaina layman was permitted to be a farmer, because agriculture meant destroying living things in the earth. In their emphasis upon non-violence (*ahiṃsā*) the Jains went to extremes unknown in other Indian religions.

Laymen were considered to be members of the Jaina order and were encouraged to live in monasteries as monks for specified periods, though they were not expected to follow the harsher austerities.

4 War

War in early India was generally accepted as being the natural activity of kings. Very few voices were raised against it and no one seems to have taken much notice of those that were. Buddhists—many of whom were of the merchant class—disapproved of war on purely economic grounds, for war has a habit of interfering with trade. Doctrines of non-violence were never applied to battles. Indeed, war was the sport of kings and was played fundamentally for glory. That there could also be profit in treasure and territory was supposed to be of secondary importance. Textbooks on statecraft naturally gave a special place to war. Most of them said that peace was a fairly simple affair, but that war needed a great deal of thought and manipulation. To this matter the *Arthaśāstra* again applied the most realistic view—a weak king was advised to keep the peace, but a strong one was to make war (though only as a last resort). The *Arthaśāstra* suggested other ways of gaining the same ends, bribery and assassination among them. If war seemed to be the only answer, however, then it was to be carried out as ruthlessly as possible. To the author, talk of chivalry and glory was both foolish and unrealistic.

The *Arthaśāstra*, however, was a textbook of aggressive imperialism, a guide to empire-building. Other texts, composed in the period of anarchy between the fall of the Mauryas and the time of the Guptas, were infected with the pessimism of the times and sought to raise what seemed to be inevitable violence into a special rite. Battle became a good thing for its own sake and a duty that no warrior could avoid. Very soon a vast body of rules for war was assembled; these included a recommendation that lives should be spared once the enemy had been put to flight. Of course, these rules were not always followed, but on the whole it seems likely that a warrior's first instinct was to keep to them and his attempts to do so may well have reduced some of the harshness of war. The wholesale looting of cities, for example, was comparatively rare in early India.

Traditionally, the army upon which the king depended in order to increase his glory was divided into four sections—cavalry, chariots, elephants, and foot-soldiers. These were the fighting elements. Behind

84 Battle scenes, episodes in the *Mahābhārata*

them was the commissariat with its wagons loaded with food and water, forage for the animals, weapons and tools and all the things necessary to keep the army fed and properly armed. Accompanying the baggage-train were men who dug trenches and constructed earthworks, carpenters, blacksmiths, and surgeons. The *Arthaśāstra* contains plans for a mobile hospital unit, complete with surgeons, nurses, drugs, and bandages, and there is evidence from other sources that such units did actually exist. There were veterinary surgeons to look after the horses and elephants. Another source also mentions women cooks. With the army went various members of the court—ministers, the royal chaplain, astrologers whose task was to work out the best time to start an attack, and some of the women of the harem.

Of the fighting divisions, the elephants played an extremely important role and one which was the subject of much theorising in military text-books. Great care was taken in the training of war-elephants. The animals were, in effect, both tank and bulldozer. They were used to smash through walls, stockades, and gates, and the enemy's infantry. They cleared a way for the army through jungle and forest. Elephants were often protected by an armour which was usually made from leather, though there are refer-ences to metal plates, and their tusks were tipped with metal spikes. As well as the mahout, each elephant usually carried two or three soldiers armed with bows, javelins, and long spears. Foot-soldiers and, on occasion, cavalry defended the animals from attack. The elephants travelled in the van of the army and were supposed to—and did—strike terror into the other side, especially if the enemy had no elephants themselves or were unused to meeting them in battle.

Unfortunately, invaders soon discovered a method of turning the elephants against their owners. However well trained, an elephant panics very easily, especially if faced by fire. One demoralised elephant very quickly transmitted its panic to the whole squadron and, trumpeting in terror, the frightened elephants threw their riders and trampled the troops of their own side. Though this must have happened many times, Indians never seemed to lose their faith in the fighting qualities of the elephant, however much they suffered as a result.

The cavalry was not usually of very high quality, either in the training or in the stamina of the horses. Another reason for the cavalry's relative lack of mobility may have been the habit of giving the horse a large drink of wine before the battle. The rider was usually protected by a breastplate and carried a lance, a sword, and sometimes a bow.

By Gupta times, the chariot had become obsolete and had probably been little used long before that. The light chariot of Vedic times gave way to a very heavy, cumbersome vehicle drawn by four horses, which carried, apart from the driver, an archer and two other soldiers. The driver, who sat on the shafts, was highly vulnerable to the enemy's arrows.

Military textbooks give very little place in their theories to the role of the foot-soldier, though obviously the infantry formed the backbone of the army. The foot-soldier was armed with a bow and a quiver of arrows, a sword and shield, and light armour. Usually, a select corps of foot-soldiers acted as the king's bodyguard.

According to most textbooks, the basic unit of the army was the *patti*, a squad consisting of one elephant, one chariot, three armoured cavalry-men, and five foot-soldiers; 21,870 *pattis*, in ascending units, were supposed to make an army. The *Arthaśāstra* talks of a unit of 45 elephants, 45 chariots, 225 horses, and 675 foot-soldiers. Five of these made a self-contained fighting unit. There is no real evidence that either of these divisions was ever strictly followed. However, Indian armies were usually very large. That of Chandragupta Maurya is said to have numbered 600,000 and Hsüan Tsang records that, at its height, Harṣa's army had 66,000 elephants and 200,000 cavalry.

The weapons of the army were those common to all the armies of the time. There were the usual pieces of artillery—a device for hurling stones, battering rams, and so on. Incendiary missiles—fire-arrows and fire-balls

—were widely used. The Indian bow usually measured six feet in length, was made from bamboo, and fired a long arrow made of cane which was frequently tipped with poison. Two-edged swords, lances, and javelins, iron maces and battle-axes were the usual weapons of the infantry.

If a fortress was to be besieged, a large camp surrounded by trenches and earthworks was set up. Each of the four sections occupied a separate part of the camp with the king and his personal followers in the centre. The camp was really more like a temporary city, with its mass of camp-followers, merchants, and prostitutes. The besieging force was supposed to starve the defenders into submission or force them to come out and fight, but fortresses were occasionally taken by storm and the technique of mining was well known.

If there was to be a battle, then very

85 A warrior with spear and sword

careful preparations were necessary. If there was sufficient time, astrologers would be busy examining omens and deciding on the most propitious day and time for the battle to start. On the evening before, special rites were carried out. Brāhmans and the king himself would address the troops, encouraging them with promises of loot and glory and the certainty that if they died in battle they would go straight to heaven. The gods were supposed to protect the king, and various prayers were said in order to ensure that they did so.

The orthodox battle-order was heavy infantry in the centre, with light infantry, chariots, and cavalry on each flank. The elephants, too, were generally concentrated in the centre while the archers were usually protected by swordsmen. The king rode in the centre of the rearguard. The battle began to the wailing of conches, the clanging of gongs, and the rumbling of drums. Soon, the ground shook with the weight of the

86 The royal bodyguard and the king in his palanquin

elephants. Swiftly moving chariots and cavalry created a vast cloud of dust through which occasionally could be seen the standards carried by the infantry.

Fighting was usually broken off when it began to get dark and started again at dawn. During the night, wounded men and animals were taken into their respective camps and given medical attention. Weapons were collected, and, if possible, repaired. After the battle had been decided, the dead were piled into mounds—each according to his caste—and cremated. Prisoners were sometimes massacred despite the disapproval of the law-givers, who were of course seldom present at battles. But such massacres were unusual. Normally, captives were released after the payment of a ransom. Those who could not pay were enslaved, but when they had paid with their labour, the amount of the ransom, they too were released.

The return of the king to his capital after a successful battle was the signal for great festivities, after which the army settled down and waited for the next war. The king and his warriors had carried out their duty—the king's to protect the state, and both to acquire glory. With this, all were satisfied except the widows and orphans of the slain, whose suffering formed the subject of some of the finest Sanskrit poems.

5 Arts and Sciences

The study of Indian art is a vast academic exercise, and there are a great many learned and semi-popular books available. Most of them frustrate the understanding of ordinary readers by over-emphasising the religious and mystical element and by maintaining that no proper appreciation of Indian art is possible without constant reference to Hindu and Buddhist religious ideas. But the only real basis on which to build any appreciation of early Indian art is the recognition that—though created under the instructions of priests and, as the centuries passed, within a framework of increasingly rigid rules for the representation of specific things—it was almost always the work of laymen. The artists and craftsmen were not priests but men who used the material world around them and the life that was lived in it as their model. It is this which gives to Indian art its

87 The distribution of the relics of the Buddha

restless vitality, which suggests not so much the world of the spirit as the world of men and their everyday life.

ARCHITECTURE

Works of secular architecture, cities, houses, and the palaces of kings, have already been mentioned (see pp. 75, 77, 109). Because perishable materials were used in their construction, little has survived to be uncovered by the archaeologist. Temples and other religious buildings, however, built in brick and stone, still stand to display both the technical achievement and the artistic vision of early Indian craftsmen.

At the beginning of the period covered by this book, the burial mound (*stūpa*) under which the remains of nobles and holy men had been placed and worshipped by the local population since Vedic times, was adopted by the Buddhists for their own purposes. The emperor Aśoka was probably responsible for the institution of stūpa-worship, and he is supposed to have distributed relics of the Buddha's body for burial in stūpas sited in the principal towns. Each relic was contained in a small casket, frequently made of carved crystal, and set in a central chamber of unburned brick. This in turn was covered with a hemisphere of burned brick and a thick layer of plaster. The dome was surmounted by an umbrella of wood or stone and was surrounded by a wooden fence screening a path around which the worshipper walked, in a clockwise direction, after entering the enclosure by the east gate.

From Maurya times until that of the Guptas, old stūpas were greatly enlarged and decorated while many new ones were built. The three most important of these were at Bhārhut, Sānchī, and Amarāvatī (see map, p. 7). At Bhārhut, the mound itself has disappeared and the best of its sculpture is now to be found in museums in India and elsewhere. Sānchī, however, remains with many of its glories undimmed by time.

In the second century BC, the stūpa at Sānchī was doubled in size and faced with stone. The wooden railing surrounding it was replaced by one in which all the details were copied in stone. About the end of the first century AD, four magnificent gateways were erected and many other buildings including some smaller stūpas were constructed around the great mound. The gateways, which resemble those at the entrances to towns, are covered with sculpture.

The simple form of the stūpa at Sānchī was soon developed into a much

88 The North Gateway at Sānchī

more ornate construction. At Amarāvatī, which was completed about AD 200, the stūpa, larger than that at Sānchī, was adorned with panels depicting the life of the Buddha. In northern India the stūpa became a much taller building, frequently set on a square platform. At Sārnāth—near Vārānasī, the site of the Buddha's first sermon—the stūpa erected in the sixth century AD was taller than its base and was constructed of patterned brick. Its high dome, cylindrical in shape, rose from a lower traditionally shaped hemisphere, with large images of the Buddha set in the gable-ends.

Apart from the stūpas, the chief surviving architecture of the period consists of artificial caves which, in the early examples, imitated the wooden construction of free-standing buildings (see p. 132). The inside of the caves is usually plain, with highly polished walls and a simple carved entrance. The method of construction—though, in fact, 'sculpture' is a more precise term—was to start at the top, cutting out and finishing the roof before working downwards. This method dispensed with the need for scaffolding. An early example of the artificial cave can be found at Bhājā in the western Deccan; it dates from early in the second century BC. The cave consists of a nave with rows of plain octagonal columns ending in a semi-circular apse in which was a stūpa cut out of the rock. Ribs of wood were originally fitted to the vaulted ceiling and the entrance was of carved wood. From these simple beginnings the cave temples with their associated monasteries developed in size and splendour. The columns of the nave became heavy with carving, and the façades of the entrances have elaborately carved stone verandas with a large central gable-window to let in the light. At Ajantā, there are twenty-seven caves cut into a horseshoe-shaped curve. These date from the second century BC to the seventh century AD.

The latest of the great cave temples were at Ellurā (some thirty miles from Ajantā) where thirty-four caves were constructed between the fifth and the eighth centuries AD. They were mainly Hindu, though there were some Buddhist and Jaina caves. Ellurā includes the great Kailāsanātha temple, dating from the second half of the eighth century, in which the surrounding rock was completely cut away to leave a free-standing temple. This method had been used before, though on a much smaller scale, at Māmallapuram on the sea coast south of present-day Madras. There, seventeen small temples were carved from outcrops of rock in the seventh century AD. The style was that of the Buddhist vihāra and the temples

89 Panorama of the Ajantā caves

were, in effect, sculptural replicas of contemporary free-standing buildings.

Nothing survives of free-standing Hindu temples from before the Gupta period. Those surviving from Gupta times are all quite small and most of them have flat roofs. Pillars are heavy, with bell-shaped capitals, and the entrances are often carved with mythological scenes and figures.

One of the finest examples of Gupta architecture is the temple dedicated to Śiva at Deogarh near Jhānsī, built either in the fifth or sixth century A D. In this temple, square-hewn masonry was held together by iron dowels. The shrine was a cube surmounted by a pyramidal tower (now ruined) which was about forty feet high. The shrine was originally surrounded by four porticos, one of which opened into the shrine itself while the others shaded panels of carving. The platform on which the temple was raised was decorated with a continuous frieze depicting events from the *Rāmāyana* which, because it represented kingly ideals, was very popular at the time.

Gupta architecture demonstrated a certain amateurishness in the technique of building free-standing structures in stone—everything is a little thicker and heavier than it need be. In fact, while looking back both to the techniques of carpentry and cave-architecture, Gupta craftsmen were making a final break with them. Indian architecture, however, never lost the sense of mass and the feeling of solidity which was the legacy of the rock-cut temple.

SCULPTURE

Between the fall of the pre-Āryan Indus cities and the time of the Mauryas, there are over a thousand years from which no work of sculpture survives to make it possible to observe the process of change. This does not mean that sculpture was not produced—only that the materials used were perishable. From the Maurya period, there remain the pillars on which the edicts of Aśoka were inscribed, the capitals of columns, and a very small number of statues. These show that there was a highly developed and traditional art in which the primary influences were Western (Persian/ Greek) in the case of the columns and pillars, and, in the case of statues, derived from the early culture of the Indus cities.

The Aśokan columns are usually of polished sandstone, about forty feet in height, surmounted by a bell-like capital and a flat slab (*abacus*) decorated with animals, wheels, and foliage, and supporting figures of lions, bulls, or elephants. The statues are somewhat heavy, and their

90 An Aśokan
capital from
Sārnāth

91 Greek columns in a sculpture from Mathurā

stylistic connection with surviving remains from the Indus cities is clearly visible.

In the second century BC the existence of a continuing tradition is observable in carvings from Bhārhut, Sānchī, and Gayā. At Bhārhut, which is probably the earliest, the reliefs tell stories of the life of the Buddha and of episodes in the *jātaka* tales, which are concerned with periods in the Buddha's previous incarnations. The treatment is realistic, but the technique seems to have been adapted from a medium other than stone, possibly from ivory, and the translation is not wholly sure. At Gayā, however, the new technique seems to have been mastered. The stone is cut much more deeply, and some of the figures, instead of being shown face on, are in three-quarters profile. At Sānchī, though there are examples of the earlier style, the great gateways are covered with sculptures of very high technical excellence, much more free and active than those of Bhārhut. At these three Buddhist shrines, the Buddha himself is represented only by such symbols as the wheel, footprints, or an empty throne.

About the first century BC a new 'school' of sculpture appeared at Mathurā, some fifty miles east of present-day Delhi. Using local

152

92 A seated Buddha from Sārnāth

white-speckled red sandstone, craftsmen produced many figures from Jaina and Buddhist legend, including representations of the Buddha himself. Perhaps the most striking remains of this school are sculptured figures of yaksas (see p. 71), frankly sensual and voluptuous, and showing quite unmistakably the Indian attitude of finding nothing odd in placing the gods in a real world. In fact, the images of the Buddha and of other divine or semi-divine figures have little of the spiritual about them. Another aspect of the Mathurā style was the telling of stories in relief panels in the form of separate episodes instead of, as at Sānchī, continuous narrative. In these panels there are many examples of Western influences—in the use of Corinthian columns, for example, of the vine leaf and the acanthus. Another roughly contemporary school, centred at Gandhāra, was considerably influenced by Rome and representations of the gods of the Greco-Roman world. It seems reasonable to assume that at Gandhāra, and possibly at Mathurā, many of the sculptors were Westerners—probably from Syria or Alexandria. The craftsmen of Mathurā and Gandhāra were patronised by the Kushan kings (see p. 15).

To the south, a more Indian style was developing. It can be seen at Amarāvatī, which lies on the banks of the river Kistnā. There, the great stūpa is decorated with carvings in the tradition of Bhārhut and Gayā but influenced by the work of sculptors in the north-west. In one sense, Amarāvatī is the apogee of the old tradition and it greatly influenced sculptors in Ceylon and south-east Asia.

The Gupta period (which is usually taken to extend from the fourth to the seventh centuries AD) is characterised by the brāhmanisation of Buddhism, a process by which a movement that began as a revolt against the religious ideas of the time was ultimately absorbed into a restatement of them. Buddhism had already, on a popular level, become a cult, with images borrowed from other cults. In Gupta times, the Buddha figure itself became serene and quiet, the image of one who has transcended all evil. The image is of a young man, with a faint smile and half-closed eyes, who is surrounded by a large halo (92). Besides stone figures, the period produced sculpture cast in bronze and copper by a process known as 'lost wax'. By this method the image is modelled in clay and then covered with a layer of wax. On top of the wax is placed another layer of clay. The wax is then melted out and metal poured into the space. After the metal has set the mould is broken and the figure inside polished. One such Buddhist image from Sultangānj is more than seven feet high, weighs about a ton,

93 A statue of the Buddha made by the 'lost-wax' method

and was probably cast in sections. Many small figures in metal survive and it was images of this type which were probably imported into China by pilgrims like Hsüan Tsang to serve as models for the Buddha-images of eastern Asia.

Portraits of the Buddha represent only a small part of the sculpture of Gupta times. Hindu gods and mythological scenes surrounded by ornamental patterns of creepers and leaves are to be found at such sites as Deogarh and represent the beginnings of the great flowering of sculpture which took place in India in mediaeval times. In the Deccan and in the south, Gupta influence can frequently be found, though there are distinct local characteristics. On the rock-cut temples at Māmallapuram (mentioned above), however, the link is with the sculpture of Amarāvatī, full of vitality and movement.

PAINTING

From literary sources we know that, in early India, palaces and the homes of the wealthy were usually decorated with mural paintings, and that painting itself was practised by both men and women of the upper classes as well as by professional artists. Temples and other religious buildings were undoubtedly decorated with wall-paintings as well as more transportable ones. Sculptures, too, were painted with colours and in gold. The surviving examples of early Indian painting, however, date only from about the first century BC. These can be found in cave 10 at Ajantā.

The murals in this cave depict stories from the *jātaka* and, like the carvings at Sānchī, relate them in continuous narrative form, no frames dividing the episodes. The representation of elephants (the story here is of the Buddha's sacrifice of his tusks during his incarnation as an elephant) is naturalistic and the space between them is filled with foliage and flowers. The technique of the artist was highly developed. There was no perspective, and distance and depth were given by placing background figures above those in the foreground. The artist used a wide vocabulary of conventions. Rocks, for example, are represented by cubes, and mountains by cubes piled upon cubes.

In the murals of Ajantā the everyday life of the times marches across the walls. There are palaces and their occupants, kings and princes, courtiers, women of the harem. There are crowds of peasants, beggars, pilgrims and ascetics, and all the animals, the birds, and the flora of the garden and the

94 Antelopes from Māmallapuram

countryside. There are other cave murals at Bāgh, 100 miles north of Ajantā, and the stylistic conventions of the Ajantā murals can be found there as well as in other and later caves.

The technique used at Ajantā was to cover the wall with a layer of clay or cow-dung, mixed with chopped straw or animal hair, and finished with a coating of fine white clay or gypsum. On to this the artist painted in bright colours, and his work was finished by a burnishing process which gave a rich lustre to the surface. In order to see what he was doing in the dark recesses of the cave, he arranged for light to be reflected from the outside by means of metal mirrors. Painting at Ajantā went on until the seventh century AD and the most famous of the paintings which survive date from the later period.

Though manuals of instruction for painters existed from about the first century AD, it was during Gupta times that the ideas governing the Indian view of art were most probably given their final form. Our principal

157

source for these ideas is the *Vishnudharmottaram*. In it, types of painting suitable for the decoration of palaces, temples, and private houses are carefully defined. The work particularly emphasises the importance of expressing emotion through movement. Another work—a commentary on the *Kāmasūtra* by Yaśodhara—as well as laying down standards for the proper presentation of moods and feelings, proportions and poses, gives instructions for the preparation of colours and ways of using the brush. Certainly, the artists of the later wall-paintings followed the advice of the treatises on art. Moods *are* expressed by specific poses and there is a profound sense of movement as the figures swirl across the walls. These paintings reflect the life of Gupta times with considerable accuracy and are extremely valuable social documents. Above all, however, they are masterpieces of the art of the painter and of the national genius, which, in the Gupta period, was so fully expressed in all the arts.

MUSIC AND DANCE

Very little is known about the development of music in India before the early centuries of the present era. Prior to this, there is rather vague evidence which indicates that the Āryans knew the seven-note scale, and a type of plain-chant used in Vedic times has been preserved by brāhmans (with probably reasonable accuracy) down to the present day.

The earliest surviving authority on the subject of music, dancing, and drama is an anonymous work of uncertain date attributed, as was the convention, to an early sage Bhārata, who was supposed to be the inventor of dramatic entertainments. This work, the *Bhārata Nātyaśāstra*, shows that music was a highly developed art and in fact differed very little from the kind of Indian music, usually called 'classical', that can be heard played by Indian musicians in the West today.

Indian music is almost more of a science than it is an art, in the sense that it is highly technical, and no really adequate treatment of it can be given here. Briefly, however, the Indian scale has seven notes, roughly corresponding to those of the European major scale. Each note can be elaborated with half and 'quarter' tones, and there are twenty-two 'quarter' tones in each octave. The use of 'quarter' tones produces a characteristic sound which, to unaccustomed ears, gives the impression that the musician is out of tune.

In addition to the scale, there are a number of types of tune. The most

95 Musicians

important of these is the *rāga*, a series of five or more notes on which a melody is constructed. Classically, six of these rāgas are assumed to be male, and there are a number of other types known as *rāginīs*, or wives of the masculine rāgas. Each of the rāgas is associated with a particular time of the day or night—dawn, morning, afternoon, and evening. There are also other associations with such emotions as joy, fear, and love.

Indian music has no harmony, and cross-rhythms and counterpoint take its place. Time is usually unlike that in European music, and very often the rhythmic figure is extremely complex. Within this framework, the Indian musician was—and remains—an improviser, probably because no true system of musical notation was developed in India. The musician, having chosen the rāga and the time, would, after perhaps playing a well-known melody based upon it, proceed to simple and then elaborate variations.

The most important of Indian instruments was the *vīṇā*, originally a ten-stringed harp played with a bow. By the end of the Gupta period, the shape had changed to that of a pear and it was played with the fingers or with a plectrum. The modern vīṇā is a later development dating from about the eighth century A D. Wind instruments included flutes and the

96 Dance poses

conch shell (see p. 67). Small drums were, as they are today, played with the fingers. Larger drums were used on festival and state occasions and there were many types of gong, bell, and cymbal.

In the dance, too, there is very little difference between that of early India and some types performed today. The Indian dance was a dramatic performance in gestures. Many of these gestures were already established in the *Bhārata Nātyaśāstra*. These included poses for the neck, the eyes, the head, and the torso. There was also a code of gestures for the hands, each one corresponding not only with a given emotion but also with gods, animals, flowers, and so on. Naturally, the practice of such highly developed arts, which required years of training, was often left to professionals, but there are references to princes and others performing the dance, and some proficiency as an instrumentalist was considered by the author of the *Kāmasūtra* to be a necessary qualification for a gentleman.

LITERATURE

The languages spoken in early India had strong class connotations. The upper classes—priests, state officials, and the rich—used Sanskrit, the language of the Āryan invaders but by now much refined. The elements of Sanskrit grammar were rigidly laid down by Pāṇini towards the end of the fourth century B C and, apart from additions to vocabulary, Sanskrit changed very little after that date. The language which Pāṇini had so carefully analysed and formulated rules for came to be called *Saṃskṛta* or 'refined'. The dialects spoken by ordinary people, which developed without the aid of a formal grammatical system, were called *Prākṛtas* or 'unrefined'. There was only one Sanskrit—the language of church and state, an upper-class lingua franca—but there were many Prākrits. One of the most important of these was *Pāli*, the religious language of Buddhism. A reasonable parallel to its use by Buddhists in contrast with the Sanskrit of the established religion can be drawn between Latin, the language of the Catholic church, and the common tongue used by the reformer, Martin Luther. In south India, non-Āryan languages—called Dravidian—were only very slowly influenced by Sanskrit. Of these languages the most important, and the one with the earliest extant literature, was Tamil.

The literature of early India follows the class division of language. The great sacred texts were in Sanskrit, as was a large body of secular literature, poetry, and drama. Prākrit was the language of the Buddhist and Jaina texts and of a small amount of secular poetry. Naturally, the various dialects were used for folk poetry and by the wandering story-teller. The class division was openly expressed in one of the principal conventions of Sanskrit drama, where more often than not the male characters of high social standing speak Sanskrit, while men of the lower classes and most women use different forms of Prākrit.

There are many surviving Sanskrit dramas, some short one-acters, others of great length with as many as ten acts. Plays were normally performed by professional actors with the minimum of properties. A curtain divided the front of the stage from the back and the actors made their entrances through it. There was no curtain between the stage and the audience. Costumes were conventional, and the audience could easily recognise what kind of character the actor was playing from his costume. The elaborate code of gestures used in the dance was also followed in dramatic performances, to conjure up moods, situations, and even material things.

Conventionally, the play would open with an invocation to one or more of the gods and the prologue, in which what was to follow was discussed by the chief actor and actress. The main body of the play was written in prose with verse interpolations. Another important convention, and one which applied to literary forms other than drama, was the absence of tragedy. All plays had to have a happy ending. The subjects ranged widely from tales of gods and heroes, comedies of life in the harem, and allegories of good and evil. In most plays there was a hero, a heroine, a villain, and a character—usually an ugly brāhman—who supplied the comic relief.

The earliest surviving plays are by the Buddhist poet, Aśvaghoṣa, who is supposed to have lived towards the end of the first century AD. These works, however, are incomplete. The oldest complete dramas are assigned to Bhāsa, but no single expert agrees with another on this author's dates —though the general opinion places him earlier than Kālidāsa, who flourished between AD 375 and 455. Of Bhāsa's work, thirteen plays survive; of Kālidāsa, the greatest of all Sanskrit dramatists, only three. Of these the most famous is *The Recognition of Sakuntala* (*Abhijñānaśakuntala*) which, when it was first translated at the end of the eighteenth century, so affected the great German dramatist Goethe that he adapted the idea of the prologue from it for his own play, *Faust*.

There were many other Sanskrit dramatists, including kings like Śudraka, Kālidāsa's contemporary, who wrote the most realistic of Sanskrit plays *The Little Clay Cart*. The emperor Harṣa also wrote three plays which have survived; two of them are harem comedies and the other on a religious theme. Some scholars believe that Harṣa's work was actually composed by others. At the very end of our period lived Bhavabhūti (early eighth century) who is second only to Kālidāsa. After him, there was a steady decline in the quality of Sanskrit drama.

The earliest surviving Sanskrit poetry is also attributed to Aśvaghoṣa and is a metrical life of the Buddha. The treatment is comparatively simple and very different from the ornate style of later Sanskrit poetry. As such poetry was written for a minority, it soon acquired highly conventional forms. Love, nature, moral conduct, were the most frequent subjects. Love-poetry was frankly erotic. Nature was used as a framework for man, and religious themes were rare.

There were numerous textbooks laying down rules for the composition of poetry. The Indian delight in careful classification and analysis is again displayed. It is unfortunate that it is not possible to make literal translations of Sanskrit verse into English; even the best versions give very little impression of the original.

Again it is Kālidāsa who is generally accepted as the greatest of Sanskrit poets. Of his surviving works, the most popular has always been the *Cloud Messenger* (*Meghadūta*). The style of the poem and its theme have been constantly imitated. The *Cloud Messenger* has 100 stanzas, but poets also liked the single stanza poem. Of this type, the finest surviving examples are by the poet Bhartṛhari, who is believed to have lived in the seventh century AD.

Sanskrit prose literature was quite a late development and it was not until the Gupta period that a distinctive style came into being. The prose narrative, highly stylised, is seen at its finest in the works of three writers, Daṇḍin, Subhandu, and Bāṇa, all of whom lived in the late sixth and early seventh centuries.

Daṇḍin's *Tales of the Ten Princes* (*Daśakumāracarita*) is a collection of tales linked together by a narrative theme. The stories are often comic and are particularly interesting for their realistic detail of the lives of thieves and prostitutes and wild tribesmen. Where Daṇḍin's prose is comparatively simple, however, Subhandu's is full of long sentences, obscure puns, and mythological allusions. In his works, the story does not count; it is the style which is everything. Bāṇa's method was very much that of Subhandu but he also provided a plot, which makes the style less heavy. Bāṇa wrote a partial life of his patron, Harṣa, with considerable accuracy, though quite a lot of exaggeration.

Another kind of prose literature was the fable. The Buddhist birth-stories—jātakas—were composed in Pāli. In these, the principal characters are frequently talking animals. A collection of Indian fables, the *Pañca-tantra* (Five Treatises), was translated into Persian in the sixth century AD and into Arabic two centuries later. From Arabic it was soon translated into many European languages and had considerable influence on Western literature.

In Tamil there is a tradition of a very ancient literature, but the surviving works cannot be earlier than the second or third centuries AD. These works consist of three poetical collections and two poetical romances. The collections deal mainly with love and war but one contains a series of moralisings. The most famous of these is the *Tirukkural*, metrical proverbs on such subjects as virtue, wealth, and sexual desire.

By the sixth century AD, Sanskrit influence had penetrated the south and the style of Tamil poetry changed, though the earliest example, *The Jewelled Anklet* (*Śilappadigāram*) is still very different in feeling from Sanskrit poetry.

TECHNOLOGY

There are many examples of high technical achievement in early India. In weaving, the products of Indian looms were of such fine quality that they found a ready market abroad, particularly in the Roman empire. Yet in pottery there was no comparable perfection. The working of stone was obviously technically advanced. The great stone columns, for example, on which the Aśokan edicts were inscribed, all came from one quarry near Vārānasī and were carved from single blocks of stone weighing up to fifty tons. Apart from the processes of cutting and polishing, the transportation of the columns over considerable distances called for high technological expertise.

India, too, had a considerable reputation for metalworking. The famous Iron Pillar of Meharauli, now a suburb of New Delhi, is twenty-three feet high. This single piece of iron, worked some time in the late fourth or early fifth century AD, has never rusted on account of its extremely high chemical purity. Unfortunately, the way in which it was made is still obscure, but the size, weight, and purity are indications of very high technical proficiency in the working of metals.

ASTRONOMY AND MATHEMATICS

Though practically nothing is known of Indian astronomical ideas in very early times, it seems probable that they were profoundly influenced by Greek astronomy in the first years of the present era, if not before. The new ideas seem to have been adopted primarily for astrological purposes. From Western astronomy, Indians acquired the signs of the zodiac as well as the seven-day week. Like all ancient astronomy, that of India was

97 The iron pillar in the courtyard of the Quwwat-ul-Islam Mosque, Meharauli

handicapped by the absence of the telescope, but Indians did have careful methods of observation and accurate systems of measurement. The only planets which could be seen with the naked eye were the sun, the moon, Mercury, Venus, Mars, Jupiter, and Saturn. Indian astronomy also gave a special place to the ascending and descending nodes of the moon.

For their calculations, Indian astronomers assumed the universe to be centred on the earth, though in the fifth century AD the astronomer Aryabhata thought the earth moved round the sun.

To Indian mathematics, the world owes the use of the zero. In early Indian inscriptions, separate symbols were used for tens and hundreds—as they are, for example, in Roman figures. But there is little doubt that nine digits and a zero had been in use by Indian mathematicians for centuries before they appeared on an inscription dated AD 698. The system was already known in Syria before this date and is specifically mentioned as being Indian by the Syrian astronomer-monk, Severus Sebokht, in 682. The inventor of the system remains one of the world's greatest unknown benefactors.

PHYSICS AND CHEMISTRY

At about the time of the Buddha (c. 563–483 BC) India had classified the elements which make up the universe as earth, air, fire, and water. A fifth element, which can be translated as 'ether', was added by some schools of thought but rejected by others. Because Indian ideas about physics were closely linked to religion they differed from sect to sect, but all maintained that the elements, except ether, were atomic, i.e. the smallest particle of matter. Buddhists also believed that the atom occupied the smallest duration of time, coming into existence and disappearing almost at once, to be replaced by another created by the first. Atoms combined in various ways according to the various schools of thought. Of course, these atomic and molecular theories were entirely theories, and not based upon experiment. The fact that they resemble modern theories is a tribute to the imagination of early Indians and nothing more. Indian physics was almost entirely based upon intuition and logic, and though there were some general theories about gravity and the expansion of solids and liquids when heated, no real attempt was made to determine any law by experimentation. In early India actual experimentation was found only in the science of acoustics.

Indian chemistry was mainly concerned with the production of medicines. Technological developments—in metallurgy, for example—were entirely the product of trial and error by craftsmen. Indian chemists were much more interested in making poisons, antidotes, and aphrodisiacs.

MEDICINE

Apart from the rather primitive medicine of the Vedas, nothing is known of the process of development between that period and the first or second century A D when the earliest surviving medical text (by Caraka) shows that a highly advanced medicine was then in common use. It would seem that Greek and Indian medicine had borrowed considerably from one another. Like the medicine of mediaeval Europe, that of India was based upon the idea of 'humours' (*doṣa*). Health was ensured by balancing the three vital humours—wind, gall, and mucus. Some schools added a fourth humour—blood.

The functioning of the body was maintained by the five winds, the first coming from the throat and making speech; the second in the heart, which was responsible for breathing and swallowing food; the third in the stomach, blowing upon the fire which was assumed to be the digestive process; the fourth in the abdomen, responsible for excretion and procreation; and, lastly, a general wind which moved the blood and the body. After digestion food went to the heart and then to the liver and became blood. Blood became flesh, then fat, bone, marrow, and semen. If the semen was not expelled it produced energy which went to the heart and was then distributed throughout the body. The process by which food underwent changes in the body was supposed to take thirty days.

Though, like other doctors in the ancient world, Indians knew very little about the body, they were aware of the existence of the nervous system. However, they had no clear idea of how the brain worked. They believed, in fact, that the heart was the centre of intelligence. This general ignorance was in the main due to prohibitions concerning the dead, which prevented dissection and the study of morbid anatomy. Nevertheless, dissection was by no means completely unknown.

Despite the lack of anatomical knowledge Indian surgery was quite advanced, its techniques acquired from actual practice. Bone-setting was highly skilled and plastic surgery was much more sophisticated than in other countries and remained so until the eighteenth century.

The profession of physician was well considered in early India. Apprenticeship was long, and physicians received authority to practise from the state. Though they did not take an oath there were very high standards of conduct laid down for the profession. Medicines were numerous. Plasters, ointments, emetics, sprays and oils, liquids and powders made from barks and roots, animals and mineral products were all part of Indian pharmacy.

167

Cow or human urine was prescribed for some diseases. There was a well-established system of dietetics. Though there was no knowledge of bacteria, and therefore no concept of asepsis, scrupulous cleanliness was insisted upon and the medicinal value of light and fresh air was well understood.

Parallel with this advanced medical science, and by no means separate from it, were magical practices. Amulets and spells were commonplace and sufferers from mental diseases were normally handed over to sorcerers. The standards of medical attention in early India probably depended very much on where you lived and on how much money you had—criteria not entirely abandoned in some countries today.

Index

The numerals in **bold type** refer to the figure-numbers of the illustrations.

Abhijñānaśakuntala (play), 162
Acrobats, 107: **63**
Administration, 44 ff.
Adultery, 38
Afghanistan, 12
Agriculture, 56, 58 ff.: **27, 28, 61**
Ahiṃsā (non-violence), 139
Ajantā, caves of, 134, 148, 156, 157: **89**
Ajātaśatru, king of Magadha, 11
Alcohol, 63
  tax on, 69
Alexander of Macedon, 12, 14
Alms-houses, 82
Amarāvatī, 146, 148, 154, 156
Amazon guards, 30: **13**
Ambapāli (courtesan), 99
Amnesty, 126
Anarchy, 4, 50
Ancestors, commemoration of, 30, 37
Āndhras, 16
Animals, draught, 109, 110: **31, 50**
  hospitals for, 82
  souls of, 74
Anklets, 85
Antelope in trap, 57: **26**
Antelopes from Māmallapuram, 156: **94**
Antiochus I, king of Syria, 13
Aphrodisiacs, 42, 166
Apsarases (female spirit musicians), 72
Arabic, 163
Arabs, 92
Archaeology, 1, 2, 4, 8, 76
Archery, 57, 99, 108
Architecture, 146 ff.: **88–91**
Areca palm, 57
Armies, private, 90
Army, the king's, 140 ff.
  camp, 143
Arrack, 57
Arthaśāstra, 2, 12, 30, 38, 40, 44, 46, 47, 50,
  52, 57, 59, 74, 90, 97, 100, 104, 141
Art gallery, 82, 100
Arts, the, 19, 94, Chapter 5
  donors, 94: **52**
Aryabhata (astronomer), 166
Āryans, 4, 5, 8, 30, 47
  religious ideas of, 6

Āryāvarta, 20
Ascetics, 28, 52, 128: **78, 79**
Aśoka, emperor, 13, 14, 42, 45, 47, 59, 76,
  82, 130, 146: **5**
  edicts of, 150, 164: **90**
Aśoka tree, 82
Aśokan columns, 150: **90**
Āśrama (life-stages), 31
Assassination, 128
Astrologers, 92, 117, 124
Astronomy, 164, 166
Asuras (evil spirits), 72
Atomic theory, 166
Avanti, 9

Bactria, 14
Bāgh, cave-paintings at, 157
Bālāditya, Gupta king, 18
Bāna (writer), 163
Banana (*kadalī*), 56, 82
Bankers, 90, 100
Barber, the king's, 116
Barley, 56
Barrel-roof, 77
Baskets, basket-makers, 27, 64: **29**
Baths, 80
Battles, 73, 143: **84**
Beans, 56
Beās river, 20
Bedroom, upper-class, 95: **53**
Beggars, professional, 84
  religious, 84, 128: **16**
Betel, 57
Bhagavad-gītā, 16
Bhājā, cave temple at, 148
Bhārata (sage), 158
Bharata tribes, 4
Bharata Nātyaśāstra, 158
Bhārhut, carvings from, 146, 152
Bhartṛhari (poet), 163
Bhāsa (author), 162
Bhavabhūti (author), 162
Bhogavatī (capital of the snake-spirits), 70
Bihār, 35, 130
Bimbisāra, 9, 11
Bindusāra, Maurya emperor, 13

Birds, 74: **69**
  cage-, 58, 80, 116, 126: **59**
Blacksmiths, 64, 65
Blood-money, 51
Blow-pipe, 57
Bows and arrows, 57
  symbolic, 126
Brāhmana, 5, 24
Brāhmanic revolts, 43
Brāhmanism, 9, 15, 69, 79, 83, 154
Brahmaputra river, 20
Bricks, 64
Brooms, 64
Brothels, 42, 101: **60**
Buddha, 9–11, 132: **83**
  carvings of, 152, 154: **3, 92, 93**
  relics of, 146: **87**
Buddhism, 3, 13, 14 ff., 19, 26, 35, 40, 43, 89,
  161
  Brāhmanisation of, 154
Buddhist monasteries, 130 ff.: **82**
Building, house-, 77 ff.
Bull, ceremonial white, 124
  fights, 108
Bullock-wagon, 62, 83: **31**
Burglary, 50
Burial mound (*stūpa*), 146: **79, 88**

Camel, Bactrian, **50**
Camphor, 92
Caraka (physician), 167
Caravans, 83, 90, 91: **50**
Cardamom, 56, 92
Carpenter, 63
Carpets, 80
Caste, 2, 5, 11, 66, 28 ff.
Cattle, 60: **28, 31**
  branding ritual, 68
Caturaṅga (board game), 97
Cavalry, 140
Cave temples, 134, 148, 156, 157: **89**
Cereals, 115
Ceremonial, 110, 112
Chaitya Hall, simulated carpentry in stone at,
  81
Champak flower, 82
Chandragupta I, 16
Chandragupta II, 16, 17, 19
  Maurya, 12, 46, 59, 80, 128, 142
Chaplain, the king's, 116
Chariots, 83, 116, 125: **67**
  builders of, 28
  war, 109, 112, 140
Chemistry, 166
Chenāb river, 20
Childbirth, 32

Childhood, 32: **14, 21, 45**
Children, 30
Chinese, 2, 16
Christians, 2, 15
Chroniclers, 1
Cinnamon, 56, 92
Cities, sacred, 74
Civil Service, 46
Classes, the four, 24 ff.
Clay, 64
Climate, 22
Clothes, 83
  of royal ladies, 120
Cock-fighting, 98
Çoins, 101
Coḷa, 16
Columns, Corinthian, 154
  of Aśoka, 150, 164: **90**
Combs, ivory, **74**
Conch, 67, 160
Concubine, **17, 76**
Conformism, 1
Consecration, the king's, 124 ff.
Cookery, 99, 103, 104, 116
Coromandel, 16
Councillors, 44, 114, 115: **67**
Court, the, 45 ff., 108 ff.: **67**
Courtesans, 42, 99, 100: **17, 60**
  accomplishments of, 99
Cows, killing of, 5, 57
  urine as medicine, 168
  veneration of, 74
Craftsmen, shortage of, 64, 65
  social standing of, 63
  taxation of, 48, 88
  village, 63, 64
Cremation, 39
Crime, 49 ff., 100
Crop rotation, 59
Curds-seller, **47**
Curfew, 50
Customs officers, 44

Daily life in the king's palace, 122 ff.
  in the town, 74 ff.
  in the village, Chapter 3
  of a man of fashion, 95 ff.: **53–58**
Dances, 160: **96**
Daṇḍin (author), 163
  Tales of the Ten Princes (*Daśakumāracarita*),
  163
Darbha (sacred grass), 78
Darius III, king of Persia, 12
Dāsa (indigenous races), 5
Date-palm, 56
Dead, disposal of the, 27, 39, 40

Death penalty, 51, 52, 126
Debt, 61
Deccan, 20, 156
Delhi, 8, 20
Demetrius, king of Bactria, 14: **6**
Demons, 72: **37**
Deodarh, temple at, 150, 156
Devadāsī (temple prostitutes), 42
Dharma Śāstras, 49
Dharma Sūtras, 49
Dice, 97: **54**
Disasters, natural, 60
Disease, 3
Divine Guardian of the Treasury, 110
Divorce, 38
Diwālī (festival of lights), 68
Dogs, 74
Drama, 18, 161, 162
Draupadi and the Five Heroes, **15**
Dravidians, 22, 161
Dressmaking, 99
Droughts, 60
Drugs, 6
Drums, 160
Drunkenness, 69
Durgā, goddess, 68
Dyes, 62, 92

Ear-rings, 85: **46**
Education, 33, 34: **14**
  of the king's heir, 127
Elephant fights, 108
  head-dress, **6**
Elephants, 74
  king's, 52, 109, 110: **64**
  sacred white, 110, 124
  war, 140 ff.
Ellurā, cave temples at, 148
Embroidery, 86, 99
Entertainers, 106, 107: **44, 62, 63**
Ethnic origins, 22
Execution, 27, 51, 52
Exports, 91, 92

Fables, 163
Fabrics, 86
Factories, state, 46
Fa-hsien (Chinese traveller), 17, 19, 52, 104
Fairies, *see Yakṣas*
Family, the, 30, 102
Famine, 3
Farms, state, 46
Fasting, 68
Ferries, 90
Fertility rites, 66, 67

Festivals, 66, 67, 106
  of lights, 68
Final life-stage (*sanyyāsin*), 32
Fines, 51
First life-stage (brahmacārin), 31
Fish, 58
Five Great Sacrifices, 37, 103
Five Heroes of *Mahābhārata*, **15**
Floods, 22, 60
Flowers, 82, 87: **48**
Flutes, 159
Food, importance in ritual, 32
  stalls, 86
  village, 55
Forced labour, 51
Foreigners (*mlecchas*), 28: **12**
Foreign guards, 128
Fruits, 56, 60
Funerals, 39
Furniture, 95: **22, 23**

Gambling, 3, 6, 95: **54**
  state control of, 46
Game, 57, 58
Games, 108
Gandhāra, sculpture at, 154: **3**
Gāndharva (marriage by consent), 37
Gandharvas (heavenly musicians), 72: **35**
Gaṇeśa, god of learning, 74
Ganges river, 8, 20, 74
Garlands, flower, 82, 87, 96: **48**
Gayā, carvings at, 152
Gāyatrī (ritual verse), 33
'General who could not be Defeated', 110
Geography, 20 ff.
Ghats, Eastern and Western, 20
Ghee, 37, 55. 115
Ghosts, 73
Ginger, 56
Girls, 67: **41**
Girnar, 59
Gladiators, 108
Gods, 43, 154
  local, 69
Gold imports, 93
'Golden Wheel', 110
Goldsmiths, 86, 114
Gondophernes, 15
Gourds, 56
Government, 44
Governors, district and provincial, 46
Grasses, sacred, 78
Greek architectural influences, 154: **91**
Greeks, 2, 12, 14, 42, 59
Gṛhastha (second life-stage), 32
Groves, 82: **43**

INDEX

Guests, 98, 103
Guilds (*śreṇi*), 89, 90
Gupta dynasty and period, 16, 18, 43, 45, 50, 64, 76, 101, 150, 154
Guru (teacher), 34

Hair curlers, **73**
Hanuman (monkey god), 74
Harbours, 94
Harem, 40, 118ff.: **71–76**
Harṣa, 19, 44, 52, 163
    signature of, **8**
Harvest, 68
Hastināpura, 8
Hemp, 6
Herdsman, 60: **28**
Hermits, 24, 39, 129ff.: **78, 79**
Hibiscus (*japā*), 82
Hills, sacred, 73
Himālayas, 20, 72, 73: **9**
Hinduism, 19, 148
Historians, lack of, 1
Holī (festival), 66
Homosexuality, 42
Horse, 60, 74, 110
    the royal, 110, 111: **66**
    sacrifice, 8, 14, 127
Hospitality, 103
Hospitals, 82, 142
Housebuilding ritual, 77ff.
Householder, the day of the orthodox, 102
    the status of the, 37
Houses, town, 76
    interiors, 80, 95
Houses, village, 54: **20, 21**
Hsüan Tsang, 35, 52, 137, 142, 156
Huns (*Hūṇas*), 18
Hunting, 57, 104: **26**

India, map of, **2**
Indo-Greek kingdoms, 14
Indra (god), 72
Indus river, 4
'Industrialists', 87
Infantry, 140ff.: **85, 86**
Iron Pillar of Meharaulī, 164: **97**
Irrigation, 48, 56, 58
Ivory, 86, 92: **74**

Jackals, 74
Jainism, 10, 12, 16, 26, 43, 138, 148, 161: **4**
Janaka, king of Videha, 8
Jātaka (Buddhist stories), 156, 157
Jāti 'caste', 29
Javelin, 57
    dancers, 107

Jester, 117
'Jewel Maiden', 110
Jewelled Anklet, The, 164
Jewelry, 85, 86, 91, 113, 114: **46**
'Jewels, The Three', 134: **82**
'Jewel that wrought Miracles', 110
Jhānsī, 150
Jhelum river, 20
Judges, the high standard expected of, 50
Jumna river, 8, 18, 74
Jungle, 53

Kailāsanātha, 148
Kālidāsa (playwright), 18, 72, 126, 162
    Cloud Messenger, 163
    The Recognition of Sakuntala, 162
Kalinga, 13
Kali-yuga (the new age), 4
Kama (god of love), 66
Kāmasūtra, 42, 95, 98, 104, 158
Kanauj, 18
Kaniṣka, 16
Karma, 6
Kāśī, 8, 11
Kāthiāwār, 16, 59
Kauṭilya, 2, 12
Keraḷa, 16, 92
Khāravela, 16
King, 8, 43, 44: **5–8, 77, 86**
    receiving tribute, **18**
King's arsenal, 114
    authority, symbols of, 76: **70**
    barber, 116
    bodyguard, 147: **86**
    chaplain, 116
    chariots, 83, 109, 112, 116: **67**
    consecration, 124ff.
    cook, 116
    councillors, 44, 45
    court, 45ff., 108ff.
    craftsmen, 113
    cup-bearer, 117
    daily life, 122
    decrees, 45
    duties, 44, 122
    elephants, 52, 109, 110: **64**
    foreign guards, 128
    gardens, 113, 116
    granary, 109
    harem, 40, 118: **13, 71–76**
    heir, 127
    horse, 110, 111: **66**
    insignia, **70**
    jester, 117
    jewellers, 113, 114
    kitchen, 115: **68**

menagerie, 109
ministers, 43: **67**
officials, 116: **19**
palace, 76, 108 ff.
    private quarters, 115
    regalia, 116: **70**
    secret passage, 115
    servants, 116
    spies, 24, 44, 46, 50, 100, 128
    stables, 109
    succession, 44
    taxation, 45, 47, 48
    treasury, 48, 113
    victorious return, 144
Kistnā river, 154
Kitchens, 44, 80: **68**
Kosala, 8, 9
Kṣatriya (warrior), 5, 24, 26, 33, 51: **85**
Kumaragupta, 18
Kuru tribe, 8
Kuruksetra, 8
Kuśa (sacred grass), 78
Kushans (Kuśānas), 15, 16, 154: **7**
Kuśinagara, 132

Lac insect, 62
Lamps, 80: **40**
Land, fertility of, 59
    ownership, 58
    settlement, inducements for, 64
Languages, 161
Law, 49
Laws of Manu, 38, 49
Leisured class, life of the, 95 ff.: **53–58**
Lentils, 56
Lesbianism, 40
Life, the Four Stages of (āśrama), 31, 32
Lighthouses, 94
Liquor, intoxicating, 6, 63, 104
    state control of, 46, 69
Literature, 1, 2, 18, 19, 98, 100, 161
Loans, 94
'Lost-wax' method of casting sculpture, 154: **93**
Lotus, 82: **42**
Love-play, 98: **55–58**

Magadha, 8, 9, 11, 12
Magic, 67, 107, 108
Magistrates, 50, 100
Mahābhārata, 8, 16, 30, 39, 123: **15, 84**
Mahāvīra, Jina (founder of Jainism), 9, 10, 11, 138: **4**
Malabar, 16, 92
Mālwā, 16
Māmallapuram, 148, 156: **94**

Man of fashion, daily life and toilet of a, 95 ff.: **53–58**
Mandasor, 18
Mangoes, 56: **24**
Manu, Laws of, 49
Marriage, 26, 35, 77
    ceremonies, 36, 37
Mariamma ('Mother of Epidemics'), 69
Masons, 64
Massage, 96, 123
Mathematics, 164
Mathurā, sculpture from, 152: **91**
Maukharis, kingdom of, 18
Maurya empire, 2, 12 ff., 43
Meat, 57, 104
Medicine, 166, 167
Megasthenes, 12, 46, 49, 75, 80, 90
Meghadūta (Cloud Messenger), 163
Meharauli, Iron Pillar of, 164: **97**
Menageries, 109
Menander, king of Bactria, 14
Mercenaries, 94, 128
Merchants, 87, 91 ff.: **52**
Mesopotamia, 4
Metalworking, 164: **97**
'Middle Way', 11
Mihirakula, king of the Huns, 18
Milestones, 90
Milk, 60, 62
Millet, 56
Mlecchas (foreigners), 28: **12**
Monasteries, 18, 35, 130 ff.: **82**
Money-lenders, 100
Monkeys, 74
Monks, Buddhist, 130, 134 ff.: **82**
    Jaina, 139
Monsoon, 22
Mural paintings, 82, 134
    at Ajantā, 156
Murder, penalties for, 51
Music, 158: **95**
Musical scale, the seven-note, 158
Muśiri, temple of Augustus at, 94
Muslim invasions, 40
Muslin, 91
Mutilation (punishment), 51
Mysore, 13

Nāga (snake spirits), 69, 70: **32**
Nāgarika (man of fashion), 95 ff.: **53–58**
Nāgasena (Buddhist philosopher), 4
Nālandā, monastery and university at, 35, 130, 137
Nanda, Mahāpadma, 11
Narbadā river, 22
Nature, the divinity of, 73

Nīlgiri Mountains, 22
Nirvāṇa, 11, 132
Non-violence (ahiṃsā), 139
Nuns, 40, 89, 136

Oil, 55, 115
    shop, 62
Old age, 39
Orissa, 16
Outcastes, 39: 12
    craftsmen, 63
Oxen, 59

Pahlava dynasty, 15
Painting, 2, 156 ff.
    manuals of, 157
Palace, 76, 108 ff.
    revolution, 123
Palanquin, 83: 86
Pāli, 161
Palmyra (town), 92
    palm, 57
Pañca Mahāyajña, 37
Pañcatantra, 163
Pāṇḍya, 16
Pāṇini, 161
Parks, 80, 82
Parricide, royal, 127
Parthians, 15
Pāṭaliputra, 11, 16, 75, 80
    Buddhist Council at, 14
Patna, 20
Patti (basic army unit), 142
Paurava (Porus), King, 12
Peacocks, 115: 69
Pearls, 92
Peas, 56, 104
Peasants, see Vaiśya, and Village
Pedlars, 62
Pepper, 56, 92
Perfumes, 62
Philosophers, 117
Physical features, 20 ff.
Physicians, 117, 167
Physics, 166
Picture galleries, 82, 100
Piety, 37
Pilgrimages, 127
Pillars, symbolic, 76
Pirates, 91
Plantain, 56
Plays, 18, 161, 162
Plough, 59: 27
Poetry, 33, 117, 162, 163
    textbooks of, 163
Police, 46, 50, 100

Polyandry, 38: 15
Polygamy, 38, 39
Ports, 91, 94
Portuguese, 28
Pottery, 64, 65: 23
Prabhākaravardhana, king, 18, 19
Prākrit (dialects), 161
Prasenajit, king of Kosala, 11
Precious and semi-precious stones, 92
Pregnancy, 105
Priests (brāhmana), 5, 6, 24: 11, 16
Princess, royal, 118, 120
    clothes and toilet, 73-75
Prisoners-of-war, 144
Prostitutes, 42, 69, 101: 17, 60
    state control of, 46
Provinces, 46
Punishments, 49, 51
Punjab, 11, 20
Purāṇas (Ancient Stories), 92
Purchase-tax, 48

Quail-fighting, 98
Questions of Milinda, 14
Quwwat-ul-Islam Mosque, 97

Rāga, Rāginī (tunes), 158, 159
Rain-making, 68
Rainy season, 22, 68, 134
Rajasthan, 11
Rākṣasas (goblins), 72
Ram-fights, 98
Rāma, 8, 44, 72, 74, 108
Rāmāyaṇa, 8, 43, 44, 74
Rams as draught animals, 109
Ransom, 144
Rāvaṇa (demon king), 72
Rāvī river, 20
Rebellion, 44
Regalia, 116: 70
Religion, 2, 5, 8-10, 23 ff.
Religious penance, 51
    ritual, see Ritual
Rest-houses, 90
Revolution, Palace, 123
Rice, 56, 59, 60, 103: 61
    flour, 104
Rig-Veda, 5, 33, 36
Ritual, childbirth and childhood, 32
    fertility, 67
    harvest, 68
    house-building, 77
    of lights (diwāli), 68
    rain-making, 68
    soil-testing, 78
    village, 65 ff.

INDEX

Rivers, 8, 18, 20, 69: **10**
  travel on, 91
Roads, 90
  prepared for the passing of the king, 124
Robbery, 50
Roman citizens, colonies of, 94
Rome, 16, 92, 93
Rope trick, 107, 108
Royal, *see* king
Rudradāman, 16, 59

Sacred cities, 74
  grasses, 78
  hills, 73
  hymns, 5
  law, 35, 37, 39, 44, 45, 49
  rivers, 73, 74
  Texts, The, 2, 5, 6, 8, 26, 27, 102: **14**
  Thread, 32, 33
  trees, 71, 73: **34**
Sacrifices, 6, 8, 14, 127
  The Five Great, 37, 103
Sakuntalā, 72
Salt, 91
Samudragupta, 16
Sānchī, 75, 146, 152, 154, 156: **33, 80, 88**
Sandalwood, 62
Sandrocottus, 12
Sanskrit, 5, 18, 20, 161, 162
Sanyyāsin (final life-stage), 32
Sārnāth, Aśokan column from, 150: **90**
  deer park at, 132
  seated Buddha from, **92**
Sātavāhanas, 16
Satī (*suttee*, widow-burning), 19, 41
Savitri (sun god), 34
Scales, 87: **30, 49**
Science, 164
Sculpture, 2, 86, 150ff.: **42, 90, 91**
Scythians (*Sakas*), 15, 16
Seals, special, 89: **1**
Seasons, 65
  festivals of, 65, 66
Second life-stage (*gṛhastha*), 32
Seleucus Nicator, 12, 14
Senāpati (general), 116
Serfs, *see* Sūdra
Sesamum, 56
'Seven Gems, The', 110: **65**
Severus Sebokht, 166
Sexual life, 41, 67, 95, 98: **17, 55–58, 60, 71, 72, 76**
Sheep, 60, 109
Shipping, 92, 94: **51**
Shops, town, 86
  village, 61, 62: **30, 47, 49**

Shrines, 127, 132, *see also* Temples
Siege, 143
Silappadigāram (*The Jewelled Anklet*), 164
Silk Road, the, 93
Sind, 11, 60
Sītā (goddess), 108
Siva (god), 68, 74, 126
  temple of, at Deogarh, 150
Skandagupta, 18, 59
Slaves, harem, 30, 116: **13, 72**
Smallpox, 69
Smoking, 105
Snake-charmers, 84, 107: **44**
Snake spirits and goddess, 69
Snakes, propitiation of, 68
Social disturbances, 4
Society, 24 ff.
Soil, ritual testing of, 76
Soma (intoxicating drink), 6, 72
Son, the importance of having a, 33
Soul, the, 6, 37
Speke, J. H., 92
Spells, 68
Spices, 56: **30, 61**
Spice trade, 92
Spies, 24, 44, 46, 50, 100, 128
Spirits, malignant, 65, 67, 70, 72: **37**
State control, 46, 69
Statues, 80: **3, 7, 92, 93**
Stockade, village, 53
Stone-working, 64, 164
Story-tellers, 2, 62
Street entertainers, 84, 107: **44, 62, 63**
Street life, town, 83 ff.
  village, 61
Students, 32, 34, 35
  at Nālandā, 137, 138
Stūpa (burial mound), 146ff., 154: **79, 88**
Şubhandu (writer), 163
Şūdra (serfs), 5, 24, 26, 27, 33, 51: **12**
Sudraka, *The Little Clay Cart* (play), 50, 162
Sugar cane, 56, 91
Sultangānj, 154
Şuṅga, Puṣyamitra, 14
Şuṅga kings, 14
Sutlej river, 18, 20
Suttee, 19, 41
Swings, 67, 95: **41**
Sword-swallowers, 107
Syria, 166

Takṣaśilā (Taxila), 11
Talipot palm, 57
Tamarind, 56
Tamil, 94, 161, 164
Tanning, 27

Tāptī river, 22
Tavern, village, 62
Taxation, 45, 47
  of country people, 61
  of craftsmen, 48, 88
  of liquor, 63, 69
Technology, 164
Temples, 76, 146
  of Augustus, 94
  of Śiva, 150
  prostitutes (devadāsi), 42
'Ten Precepts, The' (of Buddha), 135
Textiles, 86, 92
Thanesar, 18
Thomas the Apostle, 15
'Three Jewels, The' (of Buddha), 134: **82**
Threshing, 68
Tilaka (beauty spot), 62
Tirukkural (Tamil proverbs), 164
Toddy, 57
Tolls, road, 90
Toramāna (Hun king), 18
Torture, 51
Town, caste segregation in, 76
  houses, 76: **53**
  moat, 75
  parks and gardens, 80 ff.
  planning, 74
  shops, 86
  street life, 83
  walls, 75: **38, 39**
Trade, overseas, 90
Trades, 'unclean', 27
Traps, 57: **26**
Treasurer, 116
Tree, sacred, 71, 73: **34**
Trees, groves of, 82: **43**
Tungabhadra river, 22

Universal King, The, 110, 126: **65**
Universities, 18, 35, 137
Untouchables (caṇḍālas), 18, 27, 76
Upanayana (second birth), 33
Utensils, domestic, 55: **23**

Vaiśālī, 99
Vaiśya (peasants), 24, 33
Vājapeya ('drink of strength'), 127
Vākāṭakas, 18
Vampires, 73
Vānaprastha (third life-stage), 32
Vāranāsī, 8, 11, 16, 164
Varṇa (colour), 5

Vatsa, 9
Vātsyāyana, 42, 95
Vedas, the, 32–34, 37
Vedic hymns, 5
  period, 5
Vegetarianism, 17, 104, 135
Veterinary surgeons, 141
Videha, 8
Vidiśā, 14
Vidyādharas (supernatural magicians), 72: **36**
Viharas (temple-monasteries), 130, 148
Vikramāditya, 16, 17
Village, the, 47: **20**
  daily life in, Chapter 3: **25–31**
  houses and furniture, 54, 55
  quarrels, inter-, 65
  rites and festivals, 65
Vīṇā (musical instrument), 101, 159
Vindhyas, 20
Vishnudharmottaram, 157
Viṣṇu, 74
Viśvāmitra (sage), 72

War, 4, 141 ff.
  attitude to, 140
  rules of, 140
Warrior, see Kṣatriya
Watchmen, 50
Water, 58
  pot, **23**
Wealth, 95
Weapons, 143: **85**
Weavers, 86, 164
Wells, 58
Western Satraps, 16
Wharves, 94
Wheat, 56
Widow, status of, 40, 41
Widow-burning, 19
Wife, duties of, 102
Women, position of, 40, 51, 102: **21, 29, 45, 59**
Women's clothes and personal adornment, 84, 85
Woodcutters, 71
Wool, 60
Wrestling, 107: **62**

Yakṣas (gnomes, fairies), 71, 154: **24, 33**
Yaśodhara, 158
Yaśodharman, 18
Yüeh—chi peoples, 15
Yuga (age, era), 4